Devine Guidance

For

Complying with the European Medical

Device Directive (MDD)

93/42/EEC

Christopher Joseph Devine, Ph.D.

© 2011

Limit of Liability/Disclaimer of Warranty

The author has put forth his best effort in compiling the content of this book; however, no warranty with respect to material accuracy or completeness is made. Additionally, no warranty is made in regards to applying the recommendations made in this book to any business structure or environment. The advice and recommendations provided within this book may not be suitable for all business structures or environments. Businesses should consult regulatory, quality or legal professionals prior to deciding on the appropriateness of advice and recommendations made within this book. The author shall not be held liable for loss of profit or other commercial damages resulting in the employment of recommendations made within this book including; special, incidental, consequential, or other damages.

ISBN-13: 978-1468137583

ISBN-10: 1468137581

About the Author

Dr. Christopher Joseph Devine

Dr. Christopher Joseph Devine, Ph.D. is the President of Devine Guidance International, a consulting firm specializing in providing solutions for regulatory compliance, quality, supplier management, and supply-chain issues facing the medical device industry. Additionally, Dr. Devine is the author of Devine Guidance, a weekly blog focusing on the understanding of regulations mandated by the FDA and other regulatory bodies; and published by the Medical Device Summit, an *e*-magazine. Furthermore, Dr. Devine is a member of the editorial board of the Medical Device Summit. Dr. Devine has 32-years of experience in quality assurance, regulatory affairs, and program management. He is a senior member of the American Society of Quality (ASQ), a member of Regulatory Affairs Professionals Society (RAPS), a member of the Project Management Institute (PMI) and resides on several technical advisory boards. Dr. Devine received his doctorate from Northcentral University, with his doctoral dissertation entitled, "Exploring the Effectiveness of Defensive-Receiving Inspection for Medical Device Manufacturers: A Mixed-Method Study." Dr. Devine also holds a graduate degree in organizational management (MAOM) and an undergraduate degree business management (BSBM). Prior to Dr. Devine's commercial career he served proudly as a member of the United States Marine Corps.

Dedication

To my wife Connie, for her patience with me spending long hours on the computer; to Kelly, Erin, and Travis, my kids, for understanding the need for dear-ole-dad to write; to my grandson Elijah Christopher, welcome to the world; to Dr. Ron Allen who continues to mentor me and provide sound advice needed to survive in the device industry; to my dear friend Brian Ludovico – thank you for your input when I pummeled you with interpretation questions; and finally to my parents, Joseph T. & Dorothy L. Devine, although they have passed, they would be equally proud of this accomplishment.

Acknowledgements

First and foremost, I want to thank Rick and Beth Biros and the entire staff of the Medical Device Summit. They continue to give me the opportunity to publish my work in a weekly forum (Devine Guidance) in this fabulous on-line industry magazine. I would also like to recognize Sangita Viswanathan, the editor of the Medical Device Summit, for her painstaking review and editing of my weekly articles.

Introduction

The purpose of Dr. D's second book is to breakdown and analyze the requirements depicted in the 93/42/EEC, also known as the European Medical Device Directive (a.k.a. the MDD). The doctor plans to tackle each of the Articles and Annexes sequentially and hopes the readers are able to glean some useful information while enjoying the common-sense, objective, and no-nonsense approach to complying with each of the requirements. For those of you that are frequent followers of Dr. D's weekly rants, posted in The Medical Device Summit, you will recognize the often poignant prose employed by Dr. D. That being said, I really hope you enjoy the book!

"There is no such thing as minimum compliance or maximum compliance, there is just compliance."

Table of Contents

Devine Guidance for Complying with the MDD

Chapter 1 – *Devine Guidance*
the Rules

Chapter One - Dr. D's Rules

Ever since Dr. D's childhood, I have always had a major aversion to rules of any kind. After all, rules are established so creative folks, like the doctor, can bend or break them. Unfortunately, bending or breaking rules in the medical device industry can result in device manufacturers ending up in regulatory purgatory or even worse. In fact, the conveyors of the rules can really unload some serious hurt on device manufacturers not willing to adhere to their rules or intentionally take liberties in regards to their rules. That being said, the doctor has created a set of rules that should keep device organizations on the straight and narrow path of compliance. If you had the opportunity to read Dr. D's first book, you will see that the doctor has added to the rules. As you will quickly see, these rules are premised on one very simple concept, "common sense." Enjoy.

- Rule #1 - Compliance to regulations is not optional; compliance is mandatory and dictated by law.

- Rule #2 - Measuring and monitoring equipment shall be calibrated, maintained, and traceable back to a recognized standard, e.g. NIST.

- Rule #3 - Document the results of all events in writing, because if it is not documented, in writing, the event did not occur.

- Rule #4 – The FDA conducts inspections for the purpose of collecting evidence, should legal action be required; while your notified body (*remember they work for you*) conduct audits. Treat each visit accordingly.

- Rule #5 – All investigations, CAPA, Response Required SCARs, product failures, audit findings, etc. require root-cause analysis and follow-up for effectiveness of the actions pursued.

- Rule #6 – All procedures, work instructions, drawings, specifications, etc. must be written, well-documented, and controlled within a defined document control system (No napkin drawings, please).

- Rule #7 – Make sure all changes, design, process, supplier, etc. are processed through the appropriate level of verification and/or validation.

- Rule #8 – Clearly mark and segregate all non-conforming material, preferably under lock and key.

- Rule #9 – Management review is an important tool employed to gage the effectiveness of your entire organization, not just quality; so ensure all of the metrics employed to monitor your business are included into the review.

- Rule #10 – Effective design control is not an option, it is a salient requirement.

- Rule #11 – Never have your quality or regulatory organizations report into manufacturing operations, i.e., the separation of church and state rule.

- Rule #12 – Traceability is required from start to finish for everything, i.e., production, process validation, design validation, aging studies, etc.

- Rule #13 – When in doubt, read the appropriate regulation, contact your notified body, talk with your quality organization or regulatory organization, and finally yet importantly, ask for Devine Guidance.

- Rule #14 – You do not have to share the results or content of internal audits, supplier audits, or management reviews with the FDA; however, you must provide evidence that this activities are occurring.

- Rule #15 - Post-market surveillance is an important activity. Please ensure all customer complaints are actively logged, investigated to root-cause (if possible), and a response returned to the complaining organization.

- Rule #16 - Responses to MDRs should be deemed mission critical. If an organization builds a documented history of late reporting of MDRs, they can expect a visit from their friends from the agency.

- Rule #17 – Adverse events documented in the European Union (EU) require notifications be made to the Competent Authorities. The Competent Authorities take vigilance reporting seriously.

- Rule #18 - The CE marking of conformity and associated registration number belongs to a device manufacturer's notified body. Thou shalt not affix the CE Mark to unapproved product.

- Rule #19 – A major deviation noted during a notified body audit can result in the removal of the CE Mark from offending product and/or the suspension of all applications to ship product into the EU.

- Rule #20 – Devices manufacturers must select a notified body that has product-specific knowledge; and one they are comfortable working with for the long term. Remember, this is a marriage.

- Rule #20 – The notified bodies work for the device manufacturers. The notified bodies are providing a service; and they are compensated, financially, for this work.

Chapter 2 – *Overview of the MDD 93/42/EEC*

Chapter Two – Overview of the MDD

As promised, Dr. D's second book is premised on understanding the complexities of the Medical Device Directive (MDD), and specifically Council Directive 93/42/EEC. A collegium of industry experts believe that complying with the Quality System Regulation (QSR) is a relatively simple task when faced with understanding and complying with the complexities and nuances associated with the MDD. One of the perceived differences between the QSR and the MDD is the enforcement approach pursued by the FDA; and their being far-less forgiving then the notified bodies and Competent Authorities when compliance lapses occur. For some reason, a minor deviation issued by a notified body during an audit is perceived as less punitive then a Form 483 issued by the agency. In reality, multiple minor deviations issued after a notified-body audit can result in a major deviation. The issuance of a stand-alone major deviation, for a significant quality system failure, can result in a notified body pulling their CE Mark from a medical device they previously approved. Can you say, "No CE Mark equates to no product sales in Europe?" That bring said, as many of you already know, the pathway for entrance into the European Economic Community (EEC) is the affixing of the CE Mark to medical-device packaging/labeling, and in some cases, the actual medical device. The concept is surprising simple – once again repeat after Dr. D; "No CE Mark equates to no product being introduced into the European Union (EU) for sale!" Good.

Similar to Dr. D's first book, exploring the virtues and idiosyncrasies of the QSR; Dr. D will pursue the same approach in dissecting the MDD. The MDD is far more complex (Dr. D's opinion) and as a result, the good doctor penned book two reflecting my poignant writing style, coupled with flights of rodomontade (look-it-up if you must) to cover the content of the Directive thoroughly.

In Chapter 2, the doctor will present a 47,500' summary of the MDD. Why 47,500' versus the 50,000' a colloquium (look-it up) most writers invoke? Because Dr. D enjoys being different. Please read on and enjoy.

The MDD

Although the focus of this chapter and the subsequent chapters are premised on exploring Council Directive 93/42/EEC, there are actually three Directives that support medical devices within the EU. Just an FYI - the other two Directives are the: (a) the Active Implantable Medical Device (AIMD) Directive – 90/385/EEC; and (b) the In Vitro Diagnostic Device (IVD) Directive – 98/79/EC. Dr. D will cover these additional directives in future books, eventually, but before Hades freezes over – I promise.

Another FYI – just in case some of you had not emerged from your hibernaculum prior to last March, 93/42/EEC was amended by 2007/42/EC. The changes went into effect on 21 March 2010. Some of the significant changes can be found under the heading "2007/42/EC – Changes to the MDD" later in this chapter. That being said, as a Directive, the MDD is broken down into 27-Articles and 12-Annexes. In this chapter, the doctor will provide a list of the Articles and Annexes. The Articles delineated within 93/42/EEC are:

- ✓ Article 1 – Definitions, scope;
- ✓ Article 2 – Placing on the market and putting into service;
- ✓ Article 3 – Essential requirements;
- ✓ Article 4 – Free movement, devices intended for special purposes;
- ✓ Article 5 – Reference to standards;
- ✓ Article 6 – Committee on Standards and Technical Regulations;
- ✓ Article 7 – Committee on Medical Devices;
- ✓ Article 8 – Safeguard clause;
- ✓ Article 9 – Classification;
- ✓ Article 10 – Information on incidents occurring following placing of

devices on the market;
- ✓ Article 11 – Conformity assessment procedures;
- ✓ Article 12 – Particular procedure for systems and procedure packs;
- ✓ Article 12a – Reprocessing of medical devices;
- ✓ Article 13 – Decisions with regard to classification, derogation clause;
- ✓ Article 14 – Registration of persons responsible for placing devices on the market;
- ✓ Article 14a – European databank;
- ✓ Article 14b – Particular health monitoring measures;
- ✓ Article 15 – Clinical investigations;
- ✓ Article 16 – Notified bodies;
- ✓ Article 17 – CE marking;
- ✓ Article 18 – Wrongly affixed CE marking;
- ✓ Article 19 – Decision in respect of refusal or restriction;
- ✓ Article 20 – Confidentiality;
- ✓ Article 20a – Cooperation;
- ✓ Article 21 – Repeal and amendment of Directives;
- ✓ Article 22 – Implementation, transitional provisions; and finally,
- ✓ Article 23 – An applicability comment, "This directive is addressed to the Member States."

Wow, 27-Articles; if the readers think the Articles, alone, might be enough material to digest; please do not forget about the 12-additional Annexes, for your reading and ultimately compliance enjoyment. The Annexes dive into topics such as Essential Requirements, Quality System Requirements, and EC Declaration of Conformity.

Specifically, the 12-Annexes associated with 93/42/EEC are entitled:

- ✓ ANNEX I – Essential Requirements;
- ✓ ANNEX II - EC Declaration of Conformity (full quality assurance system);
- ✓ ANNEX III – EC Type-Examination;
- ✓ ANNEX IV – EC Verification;
- ✓ ANNEX V – EC Declaration of Conformity (production quality assurance);
- ✓ ANNEX VI – EC Declaration of Conformity (product quality assurance);
- ✓ ANNEX VII – EC Declaration of Conformity;
- ✓ ANNEX VIII – Statement Concerning Devices for Special Purposes;
- ✓ ANNEX IX – Classification Criteria;
- ✓ ANNEX X – Clinical Evaluation;
- ✓ ANNEX XI – Criteria to be Met for the Designation of Notified Bodies; and
- ✓ ANNEX XII – CE Marling of Conformity.

2007/42/EC – Changes to the MDD

Are you overloaded yet? The reason Dr. D is asking is that there is so much more to digest in regards to the MDD. What about all of the changes that went into effect on 21 March 2010? These changes were significant and many device manufacturers were slow in responding to these changes. Thank God, Dr. D worked for an organization that began working toward compliance 18-months in advance of these changes becoming law. Oh yes, did Dr. D mention that the MDD is actually law within the EU? The doctor wonders what color the jumpsuits, for the Chief Jailable Officer (CJO), might be in the EU? Regardless, Dr. D has taken the liberty of delineating some of the major amendments made to the MDD in March of 2010. I hope each of your organizations successfully incorporated each of the amendments into your quality systems.

1. Software as a medical device, depending on the application was added to the Directive.

2. All devices covered under the Directive now require clinical data to support product safety and efficacy (regardless of classification).

3. Custom-made devices now require inclusion into post-market surveillance activities.

4. Single-use devices, that are reused (never a good idea to reuse a single-use device), now require a risk assessment delineating performance issues and risk associated with potential reuse.

5. Instructions for Use (IFU) must be placed into an organization's document control system and managed accordingly (a.k.a., controlled document – revision control is required).

6. Post-market surveillance activities must be documented by written procedure(s), for each device, including trending activities.

7. Clinical data must be included in the technical file.

8. For manufacturers located outside of the EU, they are now required to appoint an EU Authorized Representative.

9. Medical devices, which double as a protective device for the user, must be assessed against essential requirements in accordance with 89/686/EEC, the Personal Protective Equipment Directive.

10. Medical devices that can be categorized as a machine are now required to be assessed against the essential requirements delineated within 2006/42/EC, the Machinery Directive.

11. There was a reclassification of some medical devices, depending upon indication for use. In some cases, e.g., Class IIb devices were reclassified as Class III, requiring the manufacturer to compile and submit a design dossier to their notified body for review and approval.

There are a few other changes that went into effect in March 2010. Dr. D strongly suggests reading the Directive to ensure all of the changes are understood and have been adequately addressed within your respective quality systems.

Dr. D's Rodomontade

Not wanting to state the obvious but obliged to do so, there are significant differences in the overall approach to placing product into the market in Europe and keeping it there, versus the United States. Once product is approved for distribution within the states (510(k) or PMA), it is for-the-most-part there for life, unless safety and efficacy concerns (i.e., hurting patients / too many MDRs) force a market withdraw (a.k.a., the dirty 6-letter word RECALL). Providing PMA supplements are filed when required (e.g., design changes), the Design History File (DHF) and Device Master Record (DMR) are maintained, the Quality Management System (QMS) is maintained, and letters to file are timely, device manufacturers playing in the FDA's sandbox should be fine.

The FDA's scenario is similar for initial product approvals in the EU but simply not the case for long-term maintenance. Class III products introduced into commerce in the EU require a Design Dossier to be assembled, reviewed, and approved by a notified body (similar concept to the PMA requirement). For Class IIa and IIb devices, the assembly of a Technical File is required (similar concept to the 510(k). In the good-old days, the path of conformity for Class IIa and IIb devices was self-certification. Now notified bodies are reviewing the technical files prior to granting product approvals. Another Dr. D FYI – it is strongly recommended, although not mandated by law, European Harmonized Standards be employed in the design and testing of new products. Trust me, it will save you a bunch of time when the notified bodies commence with the proverbial; "Why wasn't this standard considered questions." Once the dossiers and technical files have been approved, certificates of approval are issued (e.g., Design Examination Certificate (DEC) for a Class III device); then and only then, can the device manufacturer legally affix the CE Mark, of their notified body, onto the label of their product.

For long-term sustainment of product sales within the EU, once every three to five-years, depending on the notified body, the Design Dossiers (Class III Products) must be submitted to your notified body for review and approval. Why? Because in the EU all of the DECs issued, regardless of the notified body, have an expiration date. Now granted, the MDD does allow the extension of certificates; however, Dr. D has seldom witnessed this practice employed. Why? Because notified bodies make money reviewing design dossiers; it is not a labor of love. Additionally, technical files are required to be reviewed during the annual visit, to your manufacturing facility, by notified bodies performing their annual surveillance audits. In fact, one of the changes to the MDD requires the notified bodies to increase the sample size of technical files reviewed during each visit. Furthermore, similar to the MDRs, if vigilance reports start flooding the offices of the Competent Authorities located within each Member State, be prepared for a potential market withdraw. The Competent Authorities have the authority (that is why they are called the Competent Authority – duh, dud-duh) to ban products from entering the EU, if these products are hurting people. Finally, if your notified body pulls your organization's certificates or the certificates expire, your organization is mandated "**By Law**" to remove the CE Mark from affected product. Why? Let Dr. D repeat, the MDD is law within the EU; and to play in the EU's medical-device sandbox, compliance to their laws is mandatory.

Takeaways

Similar to the QSR, the MDD defines the framework for the levels of compliance needed for products to be distributed within the EEC. The number one takeaway from this chapter is that a CE Mark is required for product to enter the EU. To obtain a CE Mark, there are a number of steps that need to occur prior to affixing the CE Mark.

(a) Select a recognized notified body (TUV-R, BSI, DEKRA, SGS, etc. and no

Dr. D is not a paid spokesperson for these organizations). Remember this relationship is a long-term partnership; and an experienced notified body is an industry necessity needed to assist in navigating the EU regulatory arena.

(b) Establish and maintain a quality QMS that is compliant with ISO 13485 and the MDD. This should not be a problem if your organization is already compliant with the QSR. Your notified body will help with the process. Remember, the notified bodies work for you, so do not be afraid to ask for their help.

(c) Compile and submit technically accurate design dossiers and technical files to your notified body for approval. Once approval is received, ensure these files are updated regularly (e.g., harmonized and industry standards are always changing).

(d) Do not attempt to ship product into the EU until all of the certificates are received, because doing so is a violation of the Directive.

(e) Ensure an EU Authorized Representative is under written contract. A Dr. D compliance tip – the notified body will want to review this contract during their annual visit.

(f) Whenever possible, Dr. D strongly suggests the use of Harmonized Standards when designing and testing products. Use of these standards, although not compulsory, will result in fewer questions from the notified bodies and faster overall product approvals.

(e) Ensure the Declarations of Conformity are accurate before having your CJO affixing their signature. Why? It just does not reflect well on the organization when the notified body finds errors in your organization's regulatory documents that claim compliance and ask for rework.

Chapter 3 – *Article 1*
"Definitions, Scope"

Chapter Three – MDD Article 1

As Dr. D. stated in Chapter 2, the Medical Device Directive (MDD) encompasses a far more complex array of documents (my humble opinion), then the Quality System Regulation (QSR). Employing my less than aureate but somewhat colorful prose, I will begin breaking down the MDD into smaller sound-bytes in the hopes that each of you can take away a better understanding of the regulatory requirements and the potential compliance pitfalls associated with complying with the Directive. Article 1 of the scope is appropriately entitled "Definitions, scope." Guess what – that is exactly what is disseminated in this chapter, the applicability and scope of the Directive. As many of you are already aware the doctor is always attempting to proselytize (look-it up if you must) to the readers the need for ongoing compliance with regulations, regardless of the regulations being mandated by law within the United States, or in the case of the MDD, the European Union (EU). That said, please read on, and enjoy.

Welcome to the MDD

Article 1 - Definitions, scope

1. This Directive shall apply to medical devices and their accessories. For the purposes of this Directive, accessories shall be treated as medical devices in their own right. Both medical devices and accessories shall hereinafter be termed devices.

2. For the purposes of this Directive, the following definitions shall apply:

(a) 'Medical device' means any instrument, apparatus, appliance, software, material or other article, whether used alone or in combination, including the software intended by its manufacturer to be used specifically for diagnostic and/or therapeutic purposes and necessary for its proper application, intended by the manufacturer to be used for human beings for the purpose of: diagnosis, prevention, monitoring, treatment or alleviation of disease, diagnosis, monitoring, treatment, alleviation of or compensation for an injury or handicap, investigation, replacement or modification of the anatomy or of a physiological process, —control of conception, and which does not achieve its principal intended action in or on the human body by pharmacological, immunological or

metabolic means, but which maybe assisted in its function by such means;

(b) 'Accessory' means an article which whilst not being a device is intended specifically by its manufacturer to be used together with a device to enable it to be used in accordance with the use of the device intended by the manufacturer of the device;

*(c) **'In vitro diagnostic medical device means any medical device'** which is a reagent, reagent product, calibrator, control material, kit, instrument, apparatus, equipment or system, whether used alone or in combination, intended by the manufacturer to be used in vitro for the examination of specimens, including blood and tissue donations, derived from the human body, solely or principally for the purpose of providing information: concerning a physiological or pathological state, or concerning a congenital abnormality, or to determine the safety and compatibility with potential recipients, or to monitor therapeutic measures. Specimen receptacles are considered to be in vitro diagnostic medical devices. 'Specimen receptacles 'are those devices, whether vacuum-type or not, specifically intended by their manufacturers for the primary containment and preservation of specimens derived from the human body for the purpose of in vitro diagnostic examination. Products for general laboratory use are not in vitro diagnostic medical devices unless such products, in view of their characteristics, are specifically intended by their manufacturer to be used for in vitro diagnostic examination;*

*(d) **'Custom-made device'** means any device specifically made in accordance with a duly qualified medical practitioner's written prescription which gives, under his responsibility, specific design characteristics and is intended for the sole use of a particular patient. The above-mentioned prescription may also be made out by any other person authorized by virtue of his professional qualifications to do so. Mass-produced devices which need to be adapted to meet the specific requirements of the medical practitioner or any other professional user shall not be considered to be custom-made devices;*

*(e) **'Devices intended for clinical investigation'** means any device intended for use by a duly qualified medical practitioner when conducting investigations as referred to in Section 2.1 of Annex X in an adequate human clinical environment. For the purpose of conducting clinical investigation, any other person who, by virtue of his professional qualifications, is authorized to carry out such investigation shall be accepted as equivalent to a duly qualified medical practitioner;*

*(f) **'Manufacturer'** means the natural or legal person with responsibility for the design, manufacture, packaging and labeling of a device before it is placed on the market under his own name, regardless of whether these operations are carried out by that person himself or on his behalf by a third party. The obligations of this Directive to be met by manufacturers also apply to the natural or legal person who assembles, packages, processes, fully refurbishes and/or labels one or more ready-made products and/or assigns to them their intended purpose as a device with a view to their being placed on the market under his own name. This subparagraph does not apply to the person who, while not a manufacturer within the meaning of the first subparagraph, assembles or adapts devices already on the market to their intended purpose for an individual patient;*

*(g) **'Intended purpose'** means the use for which the device is intended according to the data supplied by the manufacturer on the labeling, in the instructions and/or in promotional materials;*

*(h) **'Placing on the market'** means the first making available in return for payment or free of charge of a device other than a device intended for clinical investigation, with a view to distribution and/or use on the Community market, regardless of whether it is new or fully refurbished;*

*(i) **'Putting into service'** means the stage at which a device has been made available to the final user as being ready for use on the Community market for the first time for its intended purpose;*

*(j) **'Authorized representative'** means any natural or legal person established in the Community who, explicitly designated by the manufacturer, acts and maybe addressed by authorities and bodies in the Community instead of the manufacturer with regard to the latter's obligations under this Directive;*

*(k) **'Clinical data'** means the safety and/or performance information that is generated from the use of a device. Clinical data are sourced from: clinical investigation(s) of the device concerned; or clinical investigation(s) or other studies reported in the scientific literature, of a similar device for which equivalence to the device in question can be demonstrated; or published and/or unpublished reports on other clinical experience of either the device in question or a similar device for which equivalence to the device in question can be demonstrated;*

*(l) **'Device subcategory'** means a set of devices having common areas of intended use or common technology;*

*(m) **'Generic device group'** means a set of devices having the same or similar intended uses or commonality of technology allowing them to be classified in a generic manner not reflecting specific characteristics;*

*(n) **'Single-use device'** means a device intended to be used once only for a single patient.*

3. Where a device is intended to administer a medicinal product within the meaning of Article 1 of Directive 2001/83/EC (1). That device shall be governed by this Directive, without prejudice to the provisions of Directive 2001/83/EC with regard to the medicinal product. If, however, such a device is placed on the market in such a way that the device and the medicinal product form a single integral product which is intended exclusively for use in the given combination and which is not reusable, that single product shall be governed by Directive 2001/83/EC. The relevant essential requirements of Annex I to this Directive shall apply as far as safety and performance-related device features are concerned.

4. Where a device incorporates, as an integral part, a substance which, if used separately, maybe considered to be a medicinal product within the meaning of Article 1 of Directive 2001/83/EC and which is liable to act upon the body with action ancillary to that of the device, that device shall be assessed and authorized in accordance with this Directive.

4a. Where a device incorporates, as an integral part, a substance which, if used separately, maybe considered to be a medicinal product constituent or a medicinal product derived from human blood or human plasma within the meaning of Article 1 of

Directive 2001/83/EC and which is liable to act upon the human body with action ancillary to that of the device, hereinafter referred to as a 'human blood derivative', that device shall be assessed and authorized in accordance with this Directive.

5. This Directive shall not apply to:

(a) In vitro diagnostic devices;

(b) Active implantable devices covered by Directive 90/385/EEC;

(c) Medicinal products covered by Directive 2001/83/EC. In deciding whether a product falls under that Directive or this Directive, particular account shall be taken of the principal mode of action of the product;

(d) Cosmetic products covered by Directive 76/768/EEC (1);

(e) Human blood, blood products, plasma or blood cells of human origin or to devices which incorporate at the time of placing on the market such blood products, plasma or cells, with the exception of devices referred to in paragraph 4a;

(f) Transplants or tissues or cells of human origin nor to products incorporating or derived from tissues or cells of human origin, with the exception of devices referred to in paragraph 4a;

(g) Transplants or tissues or cells of animal origin, unless a device is manufactured utilizing

6. Where a device is intended by the manufacturer to be used in accordance with both the provisions on personal protective equipment in Council Directive 89/686/EEC (1) and this Directive, the relevant basic health and safety requirements of Directive 89/686/EEC shall also be fulfilled.

7. This Directive is a specific Directive within the meaning of Article 1(4) of Directive 2004/108/EC of the European Parliament and of the Council (2).

8. This Directive shall not affect the application of Council Directive 96/29/Euratom of 13 May 1996 laying down basic safety standards for the protection of the health of workers and the general public against the dangers arising from ionizing radiation (3), nor of Council Directive 97/43/Euratom of 30 June 1997 on health protection of individuals against the dangers of ionizing radiation in relation to medical exposure (4).

Directive Applicability

Simply put, this Directive is all encompassing for medical devices except for when exclusions are noted within the Directive or when one of the other two Directives are deemed applicable. Well what in the heck does that mean Dr. D? Basically, this Directive (minus exclusions) is applicable for medical devices and their accessories. I am sure most of you are familiar with the practice of listing applicable accessory devices within your design dossiers and technical files. In fact, the listing of ancillary and accessory devices is a mandatory requirement. Additionally, you should be managing accessory-technical-data files (ATDF) as a subset to dossiers and technical files. Yes, that is a whole lot of documentation to create and manage; however, it is just part of the price of admission into the medical device market within the EU. Dr. D will let you in on a little secret, "the notified bodies will review your ATDFs as part of their annual friendly visit to your facilities; and if they are not being managed properly, your organization will receive deviations." The notified body expectation is that an ATDF should be sustained as meticulously as a standard technical file. That is also Dr. D's expectation as well, as I have spent way too-many years bringing technical files and ATDFs into compliance with this Directive.

Directive Definitions

Since the definitions provided within the Directive are for the most part self-explanatory, Dr. D is not going to dwell too much on this section of Article 1. However, there are a few definitions, changes to definitions, and new definitions, that you should be keenly aware of because of the amendments to the Directive made in March of 2010 (Directive 2007/47/EC). Some of the Dr. D watch outs are:

- Software has been added to the medical device definition;
- There were significant changes to the in-vitro diagnostics definition (a must read);
- Custom-made device inclusions into the Directive;
- Expansion of the clinical investigation requirements;
- Authorized Representative (new definition) – required for all device manufacturers located outside of the EU;
- Clinical Data (new definition) - the additional requirement for clinical data to support product submissions (clinical data must be included in dossiers and technical files);
- Device Subcategory (new definition);
- Generic Device Group (new definition); and
- Single-use device (new definition).

As the doctor previously said, the definitions are very well defined. Device manufacturers

19

just need to ensure all of the changes are understood and incorporated into their technical documentation and day-to-day activities, as appropriate.

Devices Administering a Medicinal Product (a.k.a., Combination Devices)

For devices categorized as administering a medicinal product (sections 3 and 4), the Directive establishes the need to consider and comply with two directives. Directive 2001/83/EEC delineates the requirements in regards to the medicinal aspects associated with this type of device; however, the MDD establishes the need for complying with specific Essential Requirements defined within Annex I of the MDD. The primary factors for the need to comply with Annex I are ensuring safety and performance features are achieved and sustained during the life of the product. Remember, safety and efficacy always counts.

Medicinal Product Derived from Human Blood (Combination Device)

Once again, the MDD requires the employment of two Directives to correctly assess and qualify a device. For starters, Article 1 of Directive 2001/83/EC should be employed for definition assessment of the device. If the device is correctly categorized as a *"human blood derivative,"* the device needs to be assessed in accordance with this Directive.

Directive Exclusions

The device and category exclusions delineated within this Directive are clearly depicted under Section 5 of Article 1 of the MDD. However, please keep in mind that just because a particular device is listed as an exclusion under this Directive, it will be covered under one of the other two Directives. Dr. D strongly recommends, actually Dr.

D emphatically recommends, working with your notified body to ensure devices being designed, qualified, and approved for distribution in the EU are qualified under the correct Directive; and the appropriate path for conformity in regards to applicable Annexes. Dr. D will expand on paths of conformity, device categories, etc. later in this book, so please keep reading.

Personal Protective Equipment

Since when did devices, categorized as Personal Protective Equipment (PPE), require the consideration of two Directives? Effective 21 March 2010, premised on the amendments made to the MDD, in accordance with 2007/42/EC, devices that can be categorized as PPE, require compliance with Essential Requirements delineated within this Directive and Directive 89/686/EEC. In short, this is somewhat of a regulatory double whammy, as multiple Directives need to be considered. In fact, there is a unique Essential Requirements Checklist (ERC) required for claiming conformity to the PPE Directive. So what can be construed as PPE? For example, if the healthcare facility is located in undesirable and dangerous location, somewhere within the EU, and a physician needs to wear a Kevlar vest for safety, during his or her trek to work; this bulletproof vest ***does not qualify*** as personal protective equipment under the Directive. However, if a physician in a catheter lab requires special gloves to protect his or hers hands from radiation, then these special gloves would be considered PPE in accordance with this Directive; and require health and safety requirements associated with 89/686/EEC to be achieved.

Specific Directive

Section 7 of Article 1 is a simple clause (just kidding – there is nothing simple

21

about the Directive) that identifies the MDD as a Directive within the meaning of Article

1(4) of another Directive (2004/108/EC). Directive 2004/108/EC is the governing

document for controlling electromagnetic energy and compatibility (a.k.a., EMC). The

link is being made between these Directives because capital equipment employed as a

medical device or forms an integral part of a medical device requires testing and

evaluation against the EMC Directive. For example, an RF generator employed as part of

an ablation system, for treating arrhythmias, would require EMC testing and certification.

The testing would have to include the RF Generator and the disposable catheter that

actually provides the therapy. I know, enough with all of the Directives Dr. D.

Unfortunately folks, I did not author the Directives. Remember, the doctor previously

issued a subtle warning that in his honest opinion, the MDD is far more complex than the

QSR. Just wait until I start diving into each of the Annexes, it is going to make your head

spin if you are not familiar with the MDD.

Directive Influence on other Directives – Ionizing Radiation

Exposure to ionizing radiation and the dangers to exposure continue to

problematic for healthcare workers and even the patient. That said, safety standards and

the overall protection of healthcare workers and other individuals potentially exposed to

ionizing radiation are protected, from a regulatory standpoint under the guise of Council

Directive 96/29/Euratom. The MDD shall not affect that Directive in regards to safety

standards and protection from ionizing radiation as a result of exposure during a medical

application.

Dr. D's Chapter Rodomontade

During a long-flight home one evening, in late December of 2010, I had the opportunity to sit next to an individual that was employed by a small medical device company located on the left coast. We talked at length about the trials and tribulations associated with placing product into the US market and touched on product entry into the EU. One of the concerns raised, by this individual, was the amount of work required to not only comply with the MDD; but all of the work required in preparation of that first notified body audit. Yes, it takes a substantial amount of work to achieve and sustain compliance to the MDD; however, there are ways to ease the overall pain when deciding to enter the European Market. Dr. D will share some of the free advice offered to this individual.

1. Selecting a competent Notified Body i.e., TUV-R, BSI, DEKRA, SGS (Dr. D is not a paid spokesperson for these organizations) will help organizations, large and small, navigate the regulatory waters associated with the complexities of the MDD and doing business within the EU.

2. Do not be afraid to hire consultants to assist in establishing a compliant quality system. Organizations such as Devine Guidance International, Inc. and Goode Consulting Industries (Dr. D is a paid spokesperson for Devine Guidance International) can help build the initial foundation for your quality system or install the entire system. Now granted, using consultants can be expensive; however, considering the time saved and the expertise they bring to the table, it is well-worth the dollars spent, to have professionals on board working in your best interest.

3. Ensure that once you have selected a European Authorized Representative; make sure you define the relationship in a contract. The notified bodies will ask to see

the contract during their annual audit.

4. Read the Medical Device Summit and Devine Guidance weekly. Did you know that all of the ranting of Dr. D are available at The Summit and are absolutely free to download?

Takeaways

The major takeaways from this chapter are: (a) significant changes made to the definitions of the MDD (21 March 10) should be clearly understood; (b) PPE requires a stand-alone and unique ERC; (c) depending on the application, software is now in scope of the MDD; and (d) combination devices require compliance to requirements delineated in multiple Directives. Additionally, Dr. D recommends printing out a copy of each of the Directives, mentioned in this article (a list of the Directives can be found in the Reference Section); and the reading of each Directive carefully. There is just so much information to be gleaned from these Directives. Furthermore, selecting a recognized notified body can ease the challenges associated with navigating the regulatory waters of the EU. Finally, if your organization does not have the bandwidth or resources to design and implement a quality system that complies with all aspects of the MDD, do not be afraid to hire competent consultants. In fact, you can hire Dr. D (Devine Guidance International, Inc.) Consultants are well worth the money spent.

"When choosing a Notified Body, remember to choose wisely."

Chapter 4 – *Article 2 "Placing on the Market and Putting into Service"*

Chapter Four – MDD Article 2

In this Chapter, Dr. D will dissect and provide guidance for complying with Article 2 of Council Directive 93/42/EEC concerning medical devices, a.k.a., the MDD. In the previous chapter, the doctor explained the salient requirement for a CE Mark to be affixed to the labeling of product being introduced into commerce within the European Economic Community (EEC). Additionally, Dr. D explained that device manufacturers could not arbitrarily affix the CE Mark, since the CE Mark actually belongs to the notified bodies. Does that mean once a notified body is selected, the purchase order issued, and the contract signed, device manufacturers can affix a CE Mark and start shipping product into Europe? The answer to this question would be a resounding no. That said, this chapter of the book will explain why.

The MDD – 93/42/EEC

Article 2 – Placing on the market and putting into service

Member States shall take all necessary steps to ensure that devices may be placed on the market and/or put into service only if they comply with the requirements laid down in this Directive when duly supplied and properly installed, maintained and used in accordance with their intended purpose.

Initial Steps toward Compliance

Similar to the Quality System Regulation (QSR) enforced by the FDA within the United States, the MDD is the European equivalent of the QSR required for the introduction of medical devices into the EEC. Just like the QSR, compliance with the MDD is mandated by law. For those of you that have been following the doctor for some time, Dr. D would like to remind the readers and invoke DG Rule # 1 - Compliance to regulations is not optional, it is mandatory and dictated by law. Now having established that "compliance is mandatory," Article 2 of the MDD becomes relatively easy to understand. Simply stated, Article 2 requires each of the Member States, i.e., Ireland, England, Italy, etc. to ensure that all devices entering into commerce comply with this Directive. Additionally, there is no mention of partial compliance, exclusion from compliance, maximum compliance, or similar nonsensical clauses associated with Article 2. If you really want to see the hackles raised on the back of Dr. D, try to convince me there is such a beast as partial compliance to a Directive, standard, or regulation. If partial compliance was an acceptable approach, then regulatory bodies would develop partial regulations. Does the logic make sense now? Dr. D wants to ensure that when organizations tackle the task of trying to understand and interpret the MDD, a common-sense approach is pursued versus holding the Directive in numinous (look-it up if you must) awe.

Getting Started

How does an organization start down the path of introducing product into Europe? Dr. D recommends selecting a qualified notified body. As I have stated in the previous chapter, there are some exceptional notified bodies (BSI, TUV-R, DEKRA, SGS, NSAI, etc.) capable of assisting organizations with the navigation of the regulatory waters associated with compliance to the MDD. For example, if an organization selected TUV-Rheinland (no Dr. D is not a paid spokesperson for TUV-R), once all of the requirements of this Directive are met, a CE Mark containing TUV-R's identification number 0197, could be affixed to the labeling of approved medical devices and shipped into Europe.

Once a notified body has been selected, the next step is to have the quality system evaluated against the requirements delineated within ISO 13485:2003. As I will discuss in a later in the book, compliance to this standard is mandated by the Directive, and not optional. If your organization is already complying with the QSR, a few minor tweaks are all that should be required to comply with ISO 13485. One piece of advice Dr. D would like to offer; I strongly recommend the creation of a compliance matrix that links both the QSR and the MDD to how requirements are achieved within your quality system (link each requirement to a written procedure). As your organization grows, such as expansion into the Japanese market, e.g., Ordinance 169 for Japan, the matrix can easily be expanded.

The next step is to submit technical documentation, for review, to the notified. Depending on the device classification (Class I, IIa, IIb, or III) the requirement will be the assembling of either a Technical File or a Design Dossier (Class III only). The Technical File and/or Design Dossier will contain all of the technical documentation to support compliance to the MDD, including testing performed in accordance with recognized standards, preferably (although not mandated) European Harmonized Standards. Remember, Dr. D strongly suggests the employment of Harmonized Standards when performing device-qualification testing, design-verification testing, validation testing, etc. Trust me – it will simplify the review and approval process of Tech Files and Design Dossiers. Additionally, before writing off a Harmonized Standard as not being applicable for a particular device, ensure written rational is provided documenting that the standard was considered. Now that does not mean every-single Harmonized Standard needs to be considered; however, relevant standards should always be considered. For example, EN 980:2008 delineates the symbols for labeling required for product released for distribution within the EU. Not only should this standard be considered, expect to receive a deviation from your notified body if the symbols employed on labeling are incorrect. In fact, failure to comply with this standard can result in product being quarantined by Member States. Can you say "RECALL?" Yes - once again that nasty 6-letter word has surfaced in Dr. D's writing. Seriously folks, accuracy counts in regards to device labeling.

If the medical devices, to be introduced for commerce into the EU are manufactured outside of the EU, the selection and employment of a European Authorized Representative will be required. As Dr. D has previously stated, it is very important that a signed-written agreement be in place that delineates the responsibilities of the European Authorized Representative and the legal manufacturer of the device. Having a purchase order in place will not suffice; and your notified body will take exception. Can you say where do I sign the deviation form?

Once the European Authorized Representative is onboard, the notified body has approved your quality system, the device application approved, and the Technical File or Design Dossier has been reviewed and approved (including the device labeling); certificates are ready to be issued by the notified body. For example, for a Class III device you can expect to receive a certificate that certifies that your quality system complies with ISO 13485. Additionally, (for a Class III device) you can expect to receive a Design Examination Certificate (DEC) that documents compliance with the MDD. Furthermore, your organization will be tasked with creating a European Declaration of Conformity (DoC), The DoC will contain the actual path of conformity claimed, e.g., Class III, rule 7 according to Annex IX of the MDD. The DoC contains information specific to the approved medical device such as:

1. Legal Manufacturer;

2. Manufacturing Site(s);

3. European Authorized Representative's Address;

4. Product Name;

5. List of Approved Model Numbers and Description;

6. Path of Conformity;

7. Name and Address of Notified Body, including CE Mark ID Number;

8. Date of First CE Mark; and

9. The Signature of the Chief Jailable Officer (CJO) – typically the highest-ranking regulatory affairs individual.

Finally, you can expect to receive an Annex II.3 Certificate (Full Quality Assurance System Approval) and/or an Annex V.3 (Quality System Production) from your notified body. These certificates document products approved and their manufacturing site, versus the specific MDD Annex and Article.

Dr. D's Rodomontade

For those of you that read DG on a weekly basis via the Medical Device Summit or have read the Doctor's previous book, I thank you. By now I hope each of you have reached the conclusion that Dr. D always preaches compliance. The doctor would never want to be in a position to have colleagues heap contumely on me for allowing medical device companies to pursue a path of "minimal compliance" to Directives, European, or otherwise. Why? Because - there is no such thing as minimal compliance to regulations. There is no such thing as maximum compliance to regulations. There is no such thing as partial compliance to regulations. There is only compliance. Please, please, and pretty-please with sugar on top, compliance is a concept that needs to be understood. Otherwise, placing devices onto the market in the EU, or anywhere else for that fact, will become a daunting task.

Takeaways

Are you surprised that Dr. D could be so verbose when discussing an Article that contains just one sentence? For the long-time followers of the doctor, you folks are probably not surprised, as I have been known not to know when to stop with the ranting and preaching. That said, I know the doctor may have drifted a little bit with the addition of cursory information needed to support the placement of product into the EU; however, the path to compliance commences with Article 2 (the doctor's opinion). Article 2 is eloquently simple and yet, very specific at the same time. What in the heck does that mean Dr. D? What it means is that device manufactures shall comply with the MDD if they want to sell medical devices in Europe. It does not get any simpler than this to understand. Compliance to this Directive is not optional – period! Additionally, Dr. D provided insight and guidance into some of the salient steps required to enter the EU device market. Remember, a few of the salient items required for device manufacturers, wishing to enter the EU are:

- Select and contract with a competent notified body;

- Ensure the quality system is compliant with ISO 13485:2003;

- Contract with a European Authorized Representative;

- Assemble a Technical Files and/or Design Dossier, considering and hopefully employing European Harmonized Standards;

- Verify label accuracy for products to be introduced into the EU (remember EN 980);

- Obtain all of the applicable certificates from the notified body; and

- Complete and sign the DoC.

Remember, a competent notified body can help with the specific details. Why? Because that is what medical device manufacturers, pay the notified body to do.

"No CE Mark equates to no product entry into Europe."

Chapter 5 - *Article 3*
"Essential Requirements"

Chapter Five – Article 3

Article 3 of Council Directive 93/42/EEC, a.k.a., the Medical Device Directive (MDD) establishes the essential requirements for medical devices, as delineated within Annex I of the Directive. Similar to the previous chapter, Article 3 is eloquent in its simplicity. In fact, just like Article 2, it is a one-sentence Article. Man, Dr. D enjoys the simple things in life, including regulations one can easily understand. Now granted my beliefs, in regards to regulatory compliance, have ossified over the years; however, it is still possible to teach "old dogs" or in my case "old Ph.D.'s" new tricks. For readers used to working within the realm of the Quality System Regulation (QSR), the doctor can relate to some level of alterity (look-it-up if you must) experienced, when being introduced to the MDD for the first time. That being said, I hope you enjoy reading this chapter as the doctor provides understanding and guidance for meeting essential requirements.

The MDD – 93/42/EEC

Article 3 – Essential Requirements

The devices must meet the essential requirements set out in Annex I which apply to them, taking account of the intended purpose of the devices concerned

What You Need to Know

Article 3 of the MDD establishes the essential requirements for the design and manufacturability of devices entering into the European Union (EU) for commerce, including the consideration of risk. As Dr. D stated in the opening paragraph, the concept mandated by Article 3 of the Directive is an easy one to understand. The Competent Authorities, for each Member State, want to ensure medical devices that reflect robust safety and efficacy attributes are the only ones making their way into the hands of healthcare practitioners within the EU. After all, similar to the FDA, the primary goals of the Competent Authorities in Europe is to regulate medical devices and protect public health, period. Additionally, mandating the need to establish and maintain essential requirements can be viewed as risk mitigation. That being said, Article 3 of the Directive invokes the need to comply with the following salient components. I strongly suggest that each of you read Annex I, in its entirety so you can absorb all of the requirements needed to comply with Article 3 of the Directive.

Annex I – Essential Requirements – Salient Components

I. General requirements

1. Devices designed and manufactured so they meet their intended use including the consideration of risk;

2. Device design and construction conforming with safety principles, considering the state-of-the-art;

3. Devices achieving performance expectations, including the acceptable design, manufacture and packaging;

4. Performances characteristics not adversely influencing device safety and efficacy;

5. Devices designed, manufactured, and packaged to ensure product preservation during transport and storage;

6. Weighing an undesirable side-effect, when determined to be an acceptable risk, against expected device performance; and

6a. Demonstration of conformity with clinical requirements (Annex X).

II. Requirements Regarding Design and Construction

7. Chemical, Physical, and Biological Properties;

8. Infection and Microbial Contamination;

9. Construction and Environmental Properties;

10. Devices with a Measuring Function;

11. Protection Against Radiation;

12. Requirements for Medical Devices Connected to or Equipped with an Energy Source; and

13. Information Supplied by the Manufacturer.

What You Need to Do

Establishing essential requirements is not rocket science; however, device manufacturers need to document compliance to the requirements. Can you guess where these requirements are documented? If you said the essential requirements checklist (ERC), you are correct. Difficult concept to understand right, compliance to the essential requirements is documented in the ERC. In fact, all of the device testing, from concept to product acceptance is documented within the ERC, including compliance to the quality management system requirements, risk management, product packaging, product labeling, etc. Device manufacturers are also expected to keep the ERC current. Fail to do so, and you expect to receive a deviation, when your notified body arrives for their annual friendly visit.

Additionally, although not required by the Directive, it is strongly recommended that harmonized standards be considered and hopefully employed, when qualifying medical devices. In many cases, compliance to some of the harmonized standards, i.e., EN ISO 13485:2003, EN 980:2008, EN ISO 14971:2009, is not optional. Regardless, once the ERC has been completed, it will need to be submitted to your notified body along with the Declaration of Conformity, Technical File or Design Dossier, as part of the application process. The ERC should also be categorized as a dynamic document because content will change over time as standards are revised. Remember, the ERC will be reviewed by your notified body during their annual surveillance visits and on-site audits of Technical Files. Yes – I know Dr. D may be belaboring the point of keeping the ERC current; however, it is an important concept to retain.

Finally, remember to incorporate a pointer to the ERC into each Technical File and/or Design Dossier. As a minimum, the document number for the ERC should be referenced. One final thought, countries like Australia (TGA requirement) want the standards employed for establishing compliance with essential requirements listed on the actual Declaration of Conformity (DoC). Please ensure the standards listed on the ERC and DoC match. Again, simple concept but I cannot count the number of times Dr. D has personally reviewed these documents and only to find out they do not match.

Takeaways

There are just three takeaways from this chapter that need to be retained.

1. Article 3 of the Directive establishes the need for compliance to Essential Requirements with a mandate to comply with Annex I.

2. Completion of the ERC is not optional, it is a requirement, and you are expected to keep the checklist current. Your notified body will review the checklist and issue deviations, if the information depicted is not accurate.

3. Dr. D strongly suggests employing harmonized standards. Trust me when I say, "It will make your path to compliance much easier."

Chapter 6 – *Article 4 "Free Movement, Devices Intended for Special Purposes"*

Chapter Six – Article 4

Article 4 of Council Directive 93/42/EEC, a.k.a., the Medical Device Directive (MDD) establishes the requirements for "free movement, devices intended for special purposes." Basically, Article 4 states you can move all medical devices into the European Union (EU) "free of charge, shipping is per gratis" – just kidding, but I hope Dr. D has caught your attention. All joking aside, there is some truth in the last sentence, and no, it is not the free shipping. According to Article 4, if a medical device has been assessed (by a notified body) for conformity with essential requirements and has a legally affixed CE mark, Member States cannot block the shipment of devices intended for special purposes or clinical investigational use, into the EU. In fact, Article 4 is prescriptive with pointers to Article 17 (CE marking) and Article 11 (conformity assessment procedures). In this chapter, the doctor will provide some insight needed for complying with Article 4 of the MDD. Before I dive into Article 4 of the Directive, I want to reinforce a point, previously made, in regards to employing harmonized standards. I was having dinner with a good friend of mine in early 2011, in Boston (yes – Dr. D does have friends); and he recommended that I reinforce the point that these standards are recommended. That being said, Dr. D will reiterate, "Harmonized standards are recommended." However, it is a daunting if not nearly impossible task to have a quality system approved or device approved without complying with a few of the more "popular standards," such as EN ISO 13485, EN ISO 14971, or EN 980.

The MDD – 93/42/EEC

Article 4 – Free Movement, Devices Intended for Special Purposes

1. Member States shall not create any obstacle to the placing on the market or the putting into service within their territory of devices bearing)the CE marking provided for in Article 17 which indicate they have been the subject of an assessment of their conformity in accordance with the provisions of Article 11.

2. Member States shall not create any obstacle to:

> *- devices intended for clinical investigation being made available to medical practitioners or authorized persons for that purpose if they meet the conditions laid down in Article 15 and in Annex VIII,*

> *- custom-made devices being placed on the market and put into service if they meet the conditions laid down in Article 11 in combination with Annex VIII; Class IIa, IIb and III devices shall be accompanied by the statement referred to in Annex VIII, which shall be available to the particular patient identified by name, an acronym or a numerical code.*

These devices shall not bear the CE marking.

3. At trade fairs, exhibitions, demonstrations, etc. Member States shall not create any obstacle to the showing of devices, which do not conform to this Directive, provided that a visible sign clearly indicates that such devices cannot be marketed or put into service until they have been made to comply.

4. Member States may require the information, which must be made available to the user and the patient in accordance with Annex I, point 13, to be in their national language(s) or in another Community language, when a device reaches the final user, regardless of whether it is for professional or other use.

5. Where the devices are subject to other Directives concerning other aspects and which also provide for the affixing of the CE marking, the latter shall indicate that the devices also fulfill the provisions of the other Directives.
However, should one or more of these directives allow the manufacturer, during a transitional period, to choose which arrangements to apply, the CE marking shall indicate that the devices fulfill the provisions only of those directives applied by the manufacturer. In this case, the particulars of these directives, as published in the Official Journal of the European Communities, must be given in the documents, notices or instructions required by the directives and accompanying such devices.

What You Need to Know

For starters, devices intended for use in clinical investigations or custom-made devices will be allowed entry into the EU if the requirements of Article 4 are met. Pretty simple right? Remember, qualifying devices for initial entry into the EU can sometimes be categorized as a quixotic (look-it up) pursuit, due to the unpredictability of some notified bodies and their interpretation of the Directive. Confucius says, "It is always better to pursue a cautionary approach and work toward full compliance with the MDD." As Dr. D stated in the opening paragraph, Member States cannot block entry of devices into the EU for use, providing these devices meet their stated essential requirements and have CE marks affixed.

There is an exception to the CE mark rule. Article 4 does permit the entry of devices not complying with the Directive providing such devices are properly identified as not being in compliance with the MDD. Additionally, devices in this category should never have a CE mark affixed. An example of devices falling into this category would be demonstration units being used for a tradeshow. God forbid - the world of pain Competent Authorities are capable of unleashing should devices in this category find their way into the hands of clinicians for actual patient use.

Another important requirement of Article 4 is that device manufacturers need to comply with the native-language requirement. The ongoing addition of country-specific labeling requirements continues to pose significant challenges for device manufacturers. According to Article 4 of the Directive, each Member State has the legal right to have device labeling and the Directions for Use (DFU) in their native language. Can you say stop killing trees? The doctor has personally seen DFUs turn into books as device manufacturers attempt to meet this Article 4 requirement. In fact, the device labeling requirements pose significant challenges due to the lack of available real estate on the labels. It seems like yesterday, the labeling requirement was English plus five-additional languages, then English plus-10 additional languages. Now it is English plus 18-

languages and 43-dialects (just kidding). So much for English being one of the six recognized international languages for commerce.

A couple of chapters ago, Dr. D mentioned that in some cases devices might be "*subject to other Directives*." According to Article 4 of the MDD, the concept of compliance with multiple Directives is acceptable; however, when such scenarios occur, the device manufacturer must clearly document the Directives that are applicable and provide the relevant compliance information to their notified body. Once again, your notified body can assist with providing direction for complying with the MDD. In the case of Article 4, the requirement is very specific; "*Where the devices are subject to other Directives concerning other aspects and which also provide for the affixing of the CE marking, the latter shall indicate that the devices also fulfill the provisions of the other Directives.*"

What You Need to Do

It is Dr. D's personal opinion, there are a modicum of qualified notified bodies that can help device manufacturers navigate the regulatory waters of the EU (TUV-R, BSI, DEKRA, NSAI, SGS, etc.) are excellent examples – again not a paid spokesperson). Select and partner with a recognized and qualified notified body; and entering devices into the European market may not be the proverbial "cake walk," but the process will be considerably more palatable. That being said, here is what you need to know.

(1). Remember to test, validate, qualify, etc. devices that are going to be entering into the EU for clinical investigations. This includes custom-made devices. The only way to accomplish this task is by obtaining formal device approval through your notified body, once essential requirements have been fulfilled. Once approved, you can affix the

CE mark containing your notified bodies' registration number; and commence with the shipments into the EU, after the applicable certificates have been received.

(2). Devices can be shipped into the EU without formal approval or a CE Mark; however, these devices must be clearly marked in regards to their lack of compliance to the Directive. The doctor strongly recommends working with your packaging/labeling group; when asking them to develop a label that clearly and boldly states the status of the sample devices (Reference Example 1). Please keep in mind, Dr. D is not a graphic artist or packaging engineer, so I apologize in advance for the lack of label creativity.

> **This Device is <u>Not</u> Intended for Human Use – It is a Sample Only!**
>
> **This Device <u>Does Not</u> Comply with Essential Requirements in Accordance with Council Directive 93/42/EEC**

(3). In regards to the challenges associated with meeting the multiple-language requirement, one approach is to develop a print-on-demand concept (labels and DFUs) for product sold outside of the United States. Dr. D would prefer widespread acceptability for an electronic DFU; and I recognize that industry (worldwide) needs to be more receptive of the electronic approach. Dr. D still recommends continuing with the practice of employing English plus 10, for device labeling. Just an FYI - at last count there were 27-Member States in the EU.

Takeaways

There are three salient takeaways from this chapter. Device manufactures can ship custom-made devices and investigational devices that comply with the appropriate essential requirements, into the EU, for patient use, without prejudice from Member States. Additionally, devices identified as samples, and not intended for patient use, can be shipped into the EU without CE Marks, providing the devices are clearly labeled in regards to their status. Finally, Member States, under the Directive, retain the legal right, to have devices entering into their Member State, contain labeling and DFUs reflecting their native tongue. It is Dr. D's professional opinion; the language issue will continue to be a challenge for the device industry, for the foreseeable future.

"There is no such thing as a free ride when it comes to compliance."

Chapter 7 – Article 5

"Reference to Standards"

Chapter Seven – Article 5

Article 5 of Council Directive 93/42/EEC, a.k.a., the Medical Device Directive (MDD) defines the requirement for "reference to standards." For those of you that have made it through the previous 6 chapters, you have already been exposed to Dr. D's diatribes in regards to compliance with harmonized standards. Yes, compliance to the harmonized standards is not mandated by law; however, it is important that harmonized standards appropriate for your medical device(s) be considered. Before the doctor forgets, ensure the rationale employed to explain why a standard was not used be documented, in writing. As always, Dr. D is more than happy to offer free advice as part of Devine Guidance International, Inc. and would end up with compunctious (look-it up) feelings if I failed to do so.

I know by now you must really be getting tired of reading about Dr. D and my ongoing emphasis of employing harmonized standards for product being introduced into commerce in the EU. Tough! When Dr. D needs to drive home a salient point, he has been known to become a pain in the proverbial ass. That being said, the doctor always/strongly recommends employing the harmonized standards for devices that are targeted for approval and entry into the European Market. Employing the harmonized standards will shorten the approval time, with your notified body, and significantly reduce the number of questions asked during the submission and review process. This holds especially true for Class III devices requiring the submission to, and approval of the Design Dossier by a notified body. On the flipside of the argument, device manufacturers can choose to ignore the employment of harmonized standards and invoke the "not mandated by law argument." Please let me know how that works for you. Dr. D will bet it doesn't.

The MDD – 93/42/EEC

Article 5 – Reference to Standards

1. Member States shall presume compliance with the essential requirements referred to in Article 3 in respect of devices which are in conformity with the relevant national standards adopted pursuant to the harmonized standards the references of which have been published in the Official Journal of the European Communities; Member States shall publish the references of such national standards.

2. For the purposes of this Directive, reference to harmonized standards also includes the monographs of the European Pharmacopoeia notably on surgical sutures and on interaction between medicinal products and materials used in devices containing such medicinal products, the references of which have been published in the Official Journal of the European Communities.

3. If a Member State or the Commission considers that the harmonized standards do not entirely meet the essential requirements referred to in Article 3, the measures to be taken by the Member States with regard to these standards and the publication referred to in paragraph 1of this Article shall be adopted by the procedure defined in Article 6

What You Need to Know

Article 5 begins with a pointer to the "*Journal of the European Communities; Member States*." It is important to become familiar with the journal because it contains a compiled list of harmonized standards within the European Union (EU). The journal also delineates the date a harmonized standard is first published, reference of superseded standard, and the date of cessation of presumption of conformity of a superseded standard. Just an FYI – as of this book, the last journal update was released on 18 January 2011 (2011/C 016/02). Additionally, Member States are required by the Directive to publish the references of national standards.

Once again, you can see that this is not really rocket science. The theme throughout the Directive is consistent; the presumption of compliance to essential requirements; and the MDD places a significant amount of emphasis on the recognition and employment of harmonized standards. In short, comply with a standard, and the presumption is that compliance with the essential requirements is achieved. Additionally, Article 5 also encompasses the employment and status of national standards and scenarios where a harmonized standard does not lead to compliance with essential requirements (ref. Article 3). Furthermore, if a Member State (one of 27) does not agree with the content of a standard, Article 5 provides a path for a Member State to contest their disagreements with standard content. As a good friend of Dr. D's stated, if a Member State considers a standard "sub-standard" Article 5 provides a pathway for allowing a Member State to pursue their grievance.

What You Need to Do

Not wanting to belabor a point but feeling obliged to do so, the notified bodies really prefer that harmonized standards be considered and employed whenever possible. Remember there are fabulous standards coming from organizations, other than harmonized standards. In fact, Association for the Advancement of Medical Instrumentation (AAMI) and International Safe Transit Association (ISTA) come to mind. However, Dr. D strongly recommends employing harmonized standards when qualifying devices for sale within the EU. I cannot place enough emphasis on even the simple task of considering a standard and then documenting why the standard was not employed. Remember, the goal here is to establish and comply essential requirements; otherwise, can you say no approvals for the EU?

Takeaways

For this chapter, there is just one takeaway. The notified bodies like the harmonized standards. They will make the lives of device manufacturers miserable if the manufacturers fail to embrace these same standards. As I mentioned earlier, Article 5 establishes the fact that harmonized standards are published *"in the Official Journal of the European Communities"* and *"Member States shall publish the references of such national standards."* Collectively, regulatory and quality professionals will sleep better at night knowing that their organizations are not taking exception to harmonized standards. Dr. D will sleep better at night knowing that he is preaching to the proverbial choir.

"Although not required, the use of Harmonized Standards is strongly recommended."

Chapter 8 – *Articles 6 & 7*
"Committee on Standards and Technical Regulations"

Chapter Eight – Articles 6 & 7

Articles 6 and 7, of Council Directive 93/42/EEC, a.k.a., the Medical Device Directive (MDD) delineate the requirements for "Committee on Standards and Technical Regulations." I would like to begin this chapter by talking a little bit about the importance of the Medical Device Directive (MDD). I attended the M D & M Show in February 2011; and was blessed with the opportunity to catch up with some old friends. That being said, a dear friend of mine (yes - the doctor does have a few friends) asked me, "How can Dr. D continue to write about such boring subjects such as regulations influencing the medical device industry?" The doctor's answer to the question was quite elementary and with another with question I might add, "If device manufacturers fail to embrace and understand regulations, then how can they expect to be successful in this industry?" My final answer (not for a million dollars) to the question was, "device manufacturers will not be successful if they fail to embrace regulations, and that is why I continue to write. At the end of the day, it is my goal to teach, enlighten, and occasionally entertain the readers using common sense and some levity"

That being said, one thing to remember when reading the MDD is that the document not only affects device manufacturers, it establishes the ground rules for the Member States in Europe, in regards to regulating medical devices. Another concept to remember is that decisions in the European Union (EU) are for-the-most-part made by a commission and supported by committees. This can be a daunting task when you consider a few basic facts; (1) there are now 27-Member States, and (2) each Member State has a say in the regulatory process concerning medical devices. That is the premise for this chapter's brief discussion on Articles 6 and 7. Please keep in mind, Dr. D would never offer brummagem (look-it up) advice when writing about quality and regulatory

issues facing device manufacturers; advice on picking racehorses, maybe so.

The MDD – 93/42/EEC

Article 6 – Committee on Standards and Technical Regulations

1. The Commission shall be assisted by the Committee setup by Article 5 of Directive, hereinafter referred to as 'the Committee'.

2. Where reference is made to this Article, Articles 3 and 7 of Decision 1999/468/EC (2) shall apply, having regard to the provisions of Article 8 thereof.

3. The Committee shall adopt its rules of procedure.

Article 7

1. The Commission shall be assisted by the Committee setup by Article 6(2) of Directive 90/385/EEC, hereinafter referred to as 'the Committee'.

2. Where reference is made to this paragraph, Articles 5 and 7 of Decision 1999/468/EC shall apply, having regard to the provisions of Article 8 thereof. The period laid down in Article 5(6) of Decision 1999/468/EC shall be set at three months.

3. Where reference is made to this paragraph, Article 5a (1) to (4) and Article 7 of Decision 1999/468/EC shall apply, having regard to the provisions of Article 8 thereof.

4. Where reference is made to this paragraph, Article 5a (1), (2), (4) and (6) and Article 7 of Decision 1999/468/EC shall apply, having regard to the provisions of Article 8 thereof.

What You Need to Know

Yes, the MDD can really make your head spin with all of the pointers to Articles,

Annexes, and paragraphs inserted into multiple locations throughout the Directive. You

can call it EU Legalize, you can say that the document reflects too many cooks having

their hands into the proverbial pot; however, Dr. D calls it job security as the Directive is

law in the EU just like the Quality System Regulation (QSR) is law in the United States.

Deal with it! So what should device manufacturers really understand about Articles 6 and 7 of the MDD. Dr. D's simple answer is that device manufactures only need to know Articles 6 and 7 exist. These articles, the doctor's opinion, have no bearing on the day-to-day operations of device manufacturers. These Articles influence the commission and the establishment of the committee, and the adoption of rules by the committee once established. Is this an over simplification? In Dr. D's humble opinion, no.

What You Need to Do

Nothing! No the doctor is not "bonkers." From a device manufacturer's standpoint, no action is required. Yes, the expectation is to continue to recognize and preferably employ harmonized standards whenever possible. Articles 6 and 7, influence standard oversight within the EU, but do not directly influence device manufacturers. Besides, as a device manufacturer, you do not make the rules, regardless of venue. Why? Because the regulators own the medical device sand box, and that gives them the right to make their own rules. Yes, device manufacturers can influence the rules through a number of venues; however, device manufacturers do not make them.

Takeaways

For this chapter, the takeaway is simple, read and understand Articles 6 and 7; however, do not lose sleep worrying over their impact to device manufacturers. Why? Because Articles 6 and 7 pertain to the Commission, the Committee and the establishment of rules for the oversight of standards, period.

Chapter 9 – *Article 8*

"Safeguard Clause"

Chapter Nine – Article 8

Article 8, of Council Directive 93/42/EEC, a.k.a., the Medical Device Directive (MDD)

delineates the requirements for the "Safeguard Clause." Can you say "Recall?" Folks,

"Recall" is that nasty 6-letter word that Dr. D invokes from time-to-time, versus "market

withdraw" a term that is often perceived as a kinder and gentler version of the device-

removal process. Regardless, Article 8 of the Directive is all about the removal of devices

from Member States when violations of the Directive occur (e.g., failure to meet essential

requirements, incorrect application of a standard, or any identified shortcoming with a

standard) or when devices pose a potential threat to patient health and safety. As always,

Dr. D hopes the readers understand my position of preaching compliance and are not just

attitudinizing (look-it up) for my benefit.

The MDD – 93/42/EEC

Article 8 – Safeguard Clause

*1. Where a Member State ascertains that the devices referred to in Article 4 (1) and (2)
second indent, when correctly installed, maintained and used for their intended purpose,
may compromise the health and/or safety of patients, users or, where applicable, other
persons, it shall take all appropriate interim measures to withdraw such devices from the
market or prohibit or restrict their being placed on the market or put into service. The
Member State shall immediately inform the Commission of any such measures, indicating
the reasons for its decision and, in particular, whether non-compliance with this
Directive is due to:*
> *(a) failure to meet the essential requirements referred to in Article 3;*
> *(b) incorrect application of the standards referred to in Article 5, in so far as it is
> claimed that the standards have been applied;*
> *(c) shortcomings in the standards themselves.*

*2. The Commission shall enter into consultation with the Parties concerned as soon as
possible. Where, after such consultation, the Commission finds that:*
> *(a) the measures are justified:*

> *(i)   it shall immediately so inform the Member State which took the measures
> and the other Member States. Where the decision referred to in paragraph*

1 is attributed to shortcomings in the standards, the Commission shall, after consulting the Parties concerned, bring the matter before the Committee referred to in Article 6(1) within two months if the Member State which has taken the decision intends to maintain it and shall initiate the advisory procedure referred to in Article 6(2);

(ii)   *when necessary in the interests of public health, appropriate measures designed to amend non-essential elements of this Directive relating to withdrawal from the market of device referred to in paragraph 1 or to prohibition or restriction of their placement on the market or being put into service or to introduction of particular requirements in order for such products to be put on the market, shall be adopted in accordance with the regulatory procedure with scrutiny referred to in Article 7(3). On imperative grounds of urgency, the Commission may use the urgency procedure referred to in Article7 (4); (b) the measures are unjustified, it shall immediately so inform the Member State which took the measures and the manufacturer or his authorized representative.*

3. Where a non-complying device bears the CE marking, the competent Member State shall take appropriate action against whomsoever has affixed the mark and shall inform the Commission and the other Member States thereof.

4. The Commission shall ensure that the Member States are kept informed of the progress and outcome of this procedure

What You Need to Know

The first requirement, inferred by Article 8, that device manufacturers need to know, is that when a Member State determines a device poses a risk to public health and safety, the Member State shall take all of the appropriate steps to ensure the offending device is withdrawn (RECALL – yes Dr. D loves throwing that word around). This includes ensuring the necessary steps are taken to restrict or prevent market access for non-compliant devices. Device manufacturers need to know and understand that recalls are expensive (duh, duh-duh – thank you Carlos Mencia) and the offending manufacturer can expect to take a significant hit on their profits as revenue streams are suddenly interrupted. Additionally, the Member State identifying the device/compliance issue shall notify the Commission in regards to market withdraws, supported by the data and logic driving their decision-making process. Furthermore, a device's failure to meet its essential requirements, a device manufacturer's incorrect application of standards, and/or issues with the standards themselves are all valid reasons for withdraw and the prevention of offending devices from entering or remaining on the European market.

The second requirement device manufacturers need to know is that the Commission will consult with the appropriate parties and make a determination on the validity of the decisions made by Member States. For example, if the actions pursued by a Member State are deemed to be justified, the Commission is tasked with notifying other Member States of the decisions made and actions pursued. If the root cause of an issue is actually standards related, the Commission will refer the issue to the Committee tasked with oversight of the standard(s) for resolution.

The third requirement device manufacturers need to know is that an urgency procedure exists for expediting the notification of all Member States; and the subsequent removal of devices deemed to pose a serious threat to patient health and safety. Once again, can you say "Recall?"

The final requirement, that device manufactures need to know, relates to the affixing of the CE Mark to products. If a device manufacturer has been notified of a device issue, resulting in the removal of product from the European market, the expectation is that the CE Mark be removed from the product – ASAP! Trust Dr. D when I say, "The competent authorities will make the lives of notified bodies miserable if a CE Mark, containing their registration number, is affixed to offending devices." This requirement is pretty cut and dry. If the device does not meet essential requirements, and perform as advertised in regards to intended use, the CE Mark shall be removed – period!

If the CE Mark is not removed, Article 8 of the Directive gives Member States the power and authority to pursue regulatory action against the offending device manufacturer.

What You Need to Do

Not wanting to state the obvious but obliged to do so, device manufacturers must ensure that devices are robust in their design and performance. For Europe, that includes meeting the essential requirements appropriate for the device's classification and intended use. One thing to keep in mind, the EU does have a reporting requirement for devices that cause patient injury or death. MEDDEV 2.12 rev 5 (Guidelines on a Medical Devices Vigilance System) makes for some interesting reading. Additionally, the EU now has a database for capturing Vigilance Reporting Data (Medical Devices Sector – Implementation Vigilance Competent Authorities Notification Reports). Now more than ever, it becomes almost impossible for problem devices to be confined to just one Member State. Furthermore, if a device manufacturer's notified body informs them that a CE Mark must be removed from products; they must move quickly to remove the CE Mark, with the highest sense of urgency. Why? Because failure to do so can result in a device manufacturer's entire product portfolio being blocked from entry into the EU or other markets that require compliance with European essential requirements, e.g., Canada, Australia, etc.

Takeaways

The takeaways from this chapter are pretty basic. (1) Device manufacturers must be prepared to withdraw their devices from the European Market if the devices pose a risk to patient health and safety. (2) Device manufacturers must remove all CE Marks affixed to offending product "ASAP" when asked to do so by their notified body.

Remember, the Competent Authorities will be watching. Finally, just a watch out, the EU is getting much better at collecting and organizing vigilance reporting data. That being said, device manufacturers are expected to react quickly when their devices have been identified as posing a threat to public health and safety within the EU.

"Medical devices that are not safe and effective should not be on the market. Can you say recall?"

Chapter 10 – *Article 9*

"Classification"

Chapter Ten – Article 9

Article 9, of Council Directive 93/42/EEC, a.k.a., the Medical Device Directive (MDD) delineates the requirements for "Classification." When entering a device into the European market, the path for conformity and the compliance with specific essential requirements is driven, in part, by the device classification. In fact it is Dr. D's humble opinion, ok not so humble opinion, the European approach to device classification is significantly better than the approach pursued by the FDA. The device classification is driven by the intended use of the device and augmented through the European employment of Global Medical Device Nomenclature (GMDN) codes. Additionally, device classification will drive the technical requirements in regards to the need for the compiling of a technical file or a design dossier (class III devices). Regardless, in this chapter the doctor will once again attempt to transform my garrulous (look-it up) writing into something that makes sense to the readers.

The MDD – 93/42/EEC

Article 9 – Classification

1. Devices shall be divided into Classes I, IIa, IIb and III. Classification shall be carried out in accordance with Annex IX.

2. In the event of a dispute between the manufacturer and the notified body concerned, resulting from the application of the classification rules, the matter shall be referred for decision to the competent authority to which the notified body is subject.

3. Where a Member State considers that the classification rules set out in Annex IX require adaptation in the light of technical progress and any information which becomes available under the information system provided for in Article 10, it may submit a duly substantiated request to the Commission and ask it to take the necessary measures for adaptation of classification rules. The measures designed to amend non-essential elements of this Directive relating to adaptation of classification rules shall be adopted in accordance with the regulatory procedure with scrutiny referred to in Article 7(3).

What You Need to Know

What manufacturers need to know, in regards to Article 9, is that it establishes four classes of medical devices for the purpose of defining accurate device classification in support of device application, path of conformity, applicable essential requirements, and registration within the EU. Class I being the least stringent and Class III the most. Devices categorized as Class III will require the compilation of a design dossier; and the formal review and approval of the dossier by a notified body. The lower device classifications will require a technical file. Notified bodies are now reviewing technical files versus the previously accepted path of device manufacturer's self-certification process, which was accepted by industry for years. Guess what? Device manufacturers can expect to experience elongated timeframes associated with this review and approval process for Class IIa, IIb, and definitely Class III devices, depending on the notified body. Additionally, if a device manufacturer and their notified body fail to reach an agreement in regards to device classification, the Competent Authority, tasked with providing the oversight for that particular notified body, will make the appropriate decision, "and the decision of the judges is final," sorry Dr. D felt compelled to toss in that remark. Furthermore, if a Member State believes that classification rules depicted within Annex IV require adaptation, due to technical progress, a request shall be made to the Commission to pursue necessary measures for adaptation of the classification rules. The actions pursued by the Commission in regards to amending non-essential requirements of the Directive and the adaption of classification rules "shall be adopted," and "the decision of the judges" just kidding.

What You Need to Do

Device manufacturers need to work with their notified bodies to ensure the correct device classification, in accordance with the Directive, is selected. Notified bodies should be working with device manufacturers, well in advance, identifying the appropriate application of the classification rules, the identification of essential requirements, and the appropriate path for conformity within the EU. Dr. D has always been a big proponent of selecting competent notified bodies. Although the doctor is not a paid spokesperson for the following notified bodies, TUV-R, BSI, NSAI, and TUV-SUD are well-respected organizations servicing the medical device industry. If you and your notified body disagree with a device classification, you have the right to question and understand your notified body's decision in regards to the classification. Remember, at the end of the day, the notified bodies work for you "the device manufacturers" and not the other way around; although some notified bodies tend to forget the nature of this business relationship.

Takeaways

For this chapter, there is just one takeaway. Article 9 establishes the concept of device classification and delineates the employment of four device classifications; (a) Class I, (b) Class IIa, (c) Class IIb, and (d) Class III. Remember – device classification will drive the path for conformity for devices entering the EU; and ultimately the need for compiling a technical file or a design dossier to support the application process.

"Correct device classification will drive the regulatory path for approval."

Chapter 11 – *Article 10*

"Information on Incidents Occurring Following Placing of Devices on the Market"

Chapter Eleven – Article 10

Article 10, of Council Directive 93/42/EEC, a.k.a., the Medical Device Directive (MDD) delineates the requirements for "Information on Incidents Occurring Following Placing of Devices on the Market." In short, this Article establishes the reporting requirements for incidents within the European Union, also known as vigilance reports. When a Member State becomes aware of a problem device, which has led to death or serious injury or has the potential to lead to death or serious injury of the patient or user, the event shall be documented and the appropriate investigation pursued. The approach to the reporting of device-related incidents, within the EU, has improved dramatically over the past three years, with the data now being shared with the Competent Authorities in all Member States. If a device manufacturer is placing product into the EU that is hurting or capable of hurting the patient or user they must react quickly in identifying suspect lots, notifying the users, withdrawing the product (RECALL), and completing the failure investigation. Failure to do so may result in the device manufacturer never recovering from the dégringolade (look-it-up) that will ensue from not taking prompt action.

The MDD – 93/42/EEC

Article 10 - Information on Incidents Occurring Following Placing of Devices on the Market

1. Member States shall take the necessary steps to ensure that any information brought to their knowledge, in accordance with the provisions of this Directive, regarding the incidents mentioned below involving a Class I, IIa, IIb or III device is recorded and evaluated centrally:

(a) any malfunction or deterioration in the characteristics and/or performance of a device, as well as any inadequacy in the labeling or the instructions for use which might lead to or might have led to the death of a patient or user or to a serious deterioration in his state of health;

(b) any technical or medical reason in relation to the characteristics or performance of a device for the reasons referred to in subparagraph (a) leading to systematic recall of devices of the same type by the manufacturer.

2. Where a Member State requires medical practitioners or the medical institutions to inform the competent authorities of any incidents referred to in paragraph 1, it shall take the necessary steps to ensure that the manufacturer of the device concerned, or his authorized representative, is also informed of the incident.

3. After carrying out an assessment, if possible together with the manufacturer or his authorized representative, Member States shall, without prejudice to Article 8, immediately inform the Commission and the other Member States of measures that have been taken or are contemplated to minimize the recurrence of the incidents referred to in paragraph 1, including information on the underlying incidents.

4. Any appropriate measures to adopt procedures to implement this Article shall be adopted in accordance with the regulatory procedure referred to in Article 7(2).

What You Need to Know

As a device manufacturer, you need to know that all reportable incidents, in the EU, require immediate action. This includes not only the potential market withdraw (RECALL) but the effective failure investigation into the cause of the device leading to patient or user injury or death. This includes the potential for injury or death. The focus of the subsequent investigation needs to be root cause with an outcome that supports the prevention of any recurrence of device failure in the future. It is also important to remember, Article 10 is also applicable to the labeling and Instructions for Use (IFU). If the device labeling and/or IFU were the cause of the injury or death to the patient or user, they need to be revised and corrected, as appropriate. Remember, a good failure investigation is all encompassing, so applying basic failure investigation tools such as a fault tree analysis is not optional. At the end of the day, devices should not be hurting the patient or user. When injuries or death occurs, the Competent Authorities will expect the devices to be withdrawn. Can you say that nasty 6-letter word, RECALL?

What You Need to Do

It has always been the humble opinion of Dr. D, prevention of devices problems is always the best policy. How do device manufacturers implement a good prevention program? It starts with a: (a) a good design; (b) continues with a robust approach to design and process verification and validation; (c) supported by manufacturing in an environment where the operators and inspectors are adequately trained; (d) ensuring the users are properly trained in the application of a finished medical device; and (f) maintenance of an effective post-market surveillance program to address device issues when incidents involving patient or user injury or death, are reported. Similar to the FDA's approach to MDRs and MAUDE, device manufacturers must be proactive when issues occur with their devices within the EU. Yes, Dr. D understands that there is no such thing as a medical device utopia; and devices will occasionally fail. However, depending on how device manufacturers respond will determine if they will be allowed to continue to play in the EU's medical device sandbox. One final point, the doctor mentioned in an earlier chapter, the EU does have a reporting requirement for devices that cause patient injury or death. MEDDEV 2.12 rev 5 (Guidelines on a Medical Devices Vigilance System). Additionally, the EU now has a database for capturing Vigilance Reporting Data (Medical Devices Sector – Implementation Vigilance Competent Authorities Notification Reports).

Takeaways

The key takeaway from this chapter is that there is an incident reporting system alive and well within the EU. Device manufacturers are expected to act immediately when reports of patient and user injury or death occur. This action needs to include a root-cause failure investigation and the implementation of appropriate remediation steps to prevent a recurrence of device issues in the EU. Trust Dr. D when I say, the Competent Authorities have the ability to make device manufacturers and the lives of notified extremely miserable, if devices are causing harm or can potentially cause harm in

Europe.

"Post-market surveillance and vigilance reporting is always a salient requirement."

Chapter 12 – *Article 11*
"Conformity Assessment Procedures"

Chapter Twelve – Article 11

Article 11, of Council Directive 93/42/EEC, a.k.a., the Medical Device Directive (MDD)

delineates the requirements for "Conformity Assessment Procedures." Simply put,

Article 11 aligns the actual classification of devices with the applicable Annex in order to

affix a CE mark containing the notified body's registration number. Understanding the

importance of device classification and the selection of the appropriate Annexes should

be considered mission critical for device manufacturers. Understanding the link between

device classification and the appropriate Annex is a crucial step for device manufactures

as they walk down the path toward conformity. That is why selecting a competent

notified body is important; even though some notified bodies believe they are the

omphalos (look-it up) of the medical device industry in the European Union (EU). That

being said, it is important for device manufacturers to comprehend terms such as "EC

type-examination," "EC declaration of conformity," and "EC verification," along with

the importance of Annex II through Annex VIII. In simplifying the MDD requirement,

Dr. D recommends committing one thought to memory; "There will not be any CE mark

affixation without a conformity assessment, and without the CE mark, there will be no

product entry into the EU." In fact, it does not take special powers to make the

presentiment (look-it up) that something bad will happen when device manufacturers

attempt to enter product into commerce, in the EU, without a CE mark. Pretty simple

concept, right?

The MDD – 93/42/EEC

Article 11 – Conformity Assessment

1. In the case of devices falling within Class III, other than devices which are custom-made or intended for clinical investigations, the manufacturer shall, in order to affix the CE marking, either:

(a) follow the procedure relating to the EC declaration of conformity set out in Annex II (full quality assurance); or

(b) follow the procedure relating to the EC type-examination set out in Annex III, coupled with: (i) the procedure relating to the EC verification set out in Annex IV; or (ii) the procedure relating to the EC declaration of conformity set out in Annex V (production quality assurance).

2. In the case of devices falling within Class IIa, other than devices which are custom-made or intended for clinical investigations, the manufacturer shall, in order to affix the CE marking, follow the procedure relating to the EC declaration of conformity set out in Annex VII, coupled with either:

(a) the procedure relating to the EC verification set out in Annex IV; or

(b) the procedure relating to the EC declaration of conformity set out in Annex V (production quality assurance); or

(c) the procedure relating to the EC declaration of conformity set out in Annex VI (product quality assurance). Instead of applying these procedures, the manufacturer may also follow the procedure referred to in paragraph 3 (a).

3. In the case of devices falling within Class IIb, other than devices which are custom-made or intended for clinical investigations, the manufacturer shall, in order to affix the CE marking, either:

(a) follow the procedure relating to the EC declaration of conformity set out in Annex II (full quality assurance); in this case, point 4 of Annex II is not applicable; or

(b) follow the procedure relating to the EC type-examination set out in Annex III, coupled with:

(i) the procedure relating to the EC verification set out in Annex IV; or

(ii) the procedure relating to the EC declaration of conformity set out in Annex V (production quality assurance); or

(iii) the procedure relating to the EC declaration of conformity set out in Annex VI (product quality assurance).

4. The Commission shall, no later than five years from the date of implementation of this Directive, submit a report to the Council on the operation of the provisions referred to in Article 10 (1), Article 15 (1), in particular in respect of Class I and Class IIa devices, and on the operation of the provisions referred to in Annex II, Section 4.3 second and third subparagraphs and in Annex III, Section 5 second and third subparagraphs to this Directive, accompanied, if necessary, by appropriate proposals.

5. In the case of devices falling within Class I, other than devices which are custom-made or intended for clinical investigations, the manufacturer shall, in order to affix the CE marking, follow the procedure referred to in Annex VII and draw up the EC declaration of conformity required before placing the device on the market.

6. In the case of custom-made devices, the manufacturer shall follow the procedure referred to in Annex VIII and draw up the statement set out in that Annex before placing each device on the market. Member States may require that the manufacturer shall submit to the competent authority a list of such devices which have been put into service in their territory.

7. During the conformity assessment procedure for a device, the manufacturer and/or the notified body shall take account of the results of any assessment and verification operations

which, where appropriate, have been carried out in accordance with this Directive at an intermediate stage of manufacture.

8. The manufacturer may instruct his authorized representative to initiate the procedures provided for in Annexes III, IV, VII and VIII.

9. Where the conformity assessment procedure involves the intervention of a notified body, the manufacturer, or his authorized representative, may apply to a body of his choice within the framework of the tasks for which the body has been notified.

10. The notified body may require, where duly justified, any information or data, which is necessary for establishing and maintaining the attestation of conformity in view of the chosen procedure.

11. Decisions taken by the notified bodies in accordance with Annexes II, III, V and VI shall be valid for a maximum of five years and may be extended on application, made at a time agreed in the contract signed by both parties, for further periods of a maximum length of five years.

12. The records and correspondence relating to the procedures referred to in paragraphs 1 to 6 shall be in an official language of the Member State in which the procedures are carried out and/or in another Community language acceptable to the notified body.

13. By derogation from paragraphs 1 to 6, the competent authorities may authorize, on duly justified request, the placing on the market and putting into service, within the territory of the Member State concerned, of individual devices for which the procedures referred to in paragraphs 1 to 6 have not been carried out and the use of which is in the interest of protection of health.

14. The measures designed to amend non-essential elements of this Directive by supplementing it, relating to the means by which, in the light of technical progress and considering the intended users of the devices concerned, the information laid down in Annex I Section 13.1 may be set out, shall be adopted in accordance with the regulatory procedure with scrutiny referred to in Article 7(3).

What You Need to Know

As stated in the opening paragraph, device manufacturers need to know and understand the link between device classification and appropriate Annex. Approval of the Technical Files for Class I, IIa, and IIb devices or the Design Dossiers for Class III devices, and the appropriate certificates issued by the notified body, including the manufacturer's signed Declaration of Conformity (DoC), will delineate the path of conformity within each document. This specifically includes the applicable Annexes. Your notified body can lead you through the process. Additionally, once the application for your device (Class III) has been approved, and in accordance with the Directive, the application will remain valid for a period of up to 5-years. Your notified body has the right to issue a 5-year extension; however, such extensions are a rare event indeed. Why? Because notified bodies make significant coin in performing these reviews. Can you say profit center? Furthermore, the Competent Authority has the power and authority to permit entry of devices into their Member State, when device manufacturers have failed to meet paragraphs 1 through 6 of Article 11. Although this is also a rare event, sometimes such decisions are in the best interest of protecting the public's health.

What You Need to Do

Device manufacturers need to continue with the reading of this fine book, while remembering Dr. D will never steer the readers in the wrong direction (at least not intentionally). All kidding aside, understanding the link between device classification and the applicable Annexes should be considered mission critical. I know Dr. D sounds like a broken record or should I say CD. Another point the doctor would like to make is in regards to Class III devices. Your notified body will perform and in-depth review of your application and the Design Dossier prior to issuing an approval and the appropriate certificates (e.g., Design Examination Certificate). Be prepared for several rounds of questions, premised on the notified body, especially if this is a new application. Depending on the notified body, the length of the approval period will be from 3 to 5-years. If during this time period, the specific device has an impeccable performance record (safe and effective); and there is no history of serious injury or death, you can always ask your notified body for an extension. All Dr. D can say is, "good luck with the request;" however, it is a device manufacturer's right to ask. Years ago, Class I and II devices were typically approved through a path of self-certification; however, notified body are now reviewing Technical Files with the same rigor employed when reviewing Design Dossiers. In fact, the notified bodies, under changes to the MDD that were made in 2010, are now required to perform a mandatory review of Technical Files during their annual audit. The sample size of Technical Files reviewed has also increased substantially. The moral of the story here is quite simple; "Technical Files should be managed and sustained accordingly to ensure they are always in a state of compliance." Finally, and the doctor cannot emphasize this point enough, device manufacturers should select a notified body they are comfortable working with, for a very-long period of time. The relationship between the manufacturer and notified body is very similar to a marriage, except the device manufacturer is paying for the pain (just kidding). Seriously, the doctor has been involved in switching to a new notified body when dozens of device were involved. Folks, it is an expensive proposition to change notified bodies. The application and reviews are the easy part, the labeling changes to incorporate the new CE mark is costly.

Takeaways

In the eyes of Dr. D, there are three important takeaways from this chapter.

1. Broken-record time - device manufacturers need to understand the link between device classification and the appropriate Annexes.

2. Notified bodies are permitted to grant application extensions for up to 5-years.

3. The Competent Authority, for a Member State, has the authority to grant device entry even if compliance to paragraphs 1 through 6 of Article 11 has not been achieved.

Chapter 13 – *Article 12 "Particular Procedure for Systems and Procedure Packs and Procedure for Sterilization"*

Chapter Thirteen – Article 12

Article 12, of Council Directive 93/42/EEC, a.k.a., the Medical Device Directive (MDD) delineates the requirements for "Particular Procedure for Systems and Procedure Packs and Procedure for Sterilization Conformity Assessment Procedures." Article 12 is all about declarations and compliance with Annex II (EC Declaration of Conformity – Full Quality Assurance System) and Annex V (EC Declaration of Conformity – Production Quality Assurance). Systems and procedure packs, being introduced into the European Union (EU) for commerce, require a written declaration, by the manufacturer, stating compliance to the requirements outlined in Article 12. The device manufacturer's Chief Jailable Officer (CJO) or an assigned and competent delegate (that looks good in an orange jumpsuit); should be the duly charged with the task of signing the declarations. Additionally, the sterilization facility employed to perform the sterilization on the systems or procedure packs is expected to sustain a recognizable quality system in accordance with Annex II or Annex V of the MDD. That being said, the organization performing the sterilization is also duly tasked with creating a signed declaration delineating compliance with the manufacturer's specifications. Dr. D would like to make a point, "Competent and qualified sterilization facilities will have an effective quality management system when such systems are approved by a recognized notified body." Finally, when devices from multiple manufacturers are included in procedure packs, Section 13 (Information Supplied by the Manufacturer) of Annex I (Essential Requirements) will apply. In short, device manufacturers need to control all of the devices being placed into the procedure packs. One final thought, remember to hold onto all of the declarations collected. Why - because these declarations need to be kept, *"at the disposal of the competent authorities."* The minimum length of retention will be 5-years.

As with all chapters of this book, Dr. D can never be accused of being farouche (look-it

up).

The MDD – 93/42/EEC

Article 12 – Particular Procedure for Systems and Procedure Packs and Procedure for Sterilization

1. By way of derogation from Article 11 this Article shall apply to systems and procedure packs.

2. Any natural or legal person who puts devices bearing the CE marking together within their intended purpose and within the limits of use specified by their manufacturers, in order to place them on the market as a system or procedure pack, shall draw up a declaration by which he states that:

> *(a) he has verified the, mutual compatibility of the devices in accordance with the manufacturers' instructions and has carried out his operations in accordance with these instructions; and*
> *(b) he has packaged the system or procedure pack and supplied relevant information to users incorporating relevant instructions from the manufacturers; and*
> *(c) the whole activity is subjected to appropriate methods of internal control and inspection. Where the conditions above are not met, as in cases where the system or procedure pack incorporate devices which do not bear a CE marking or where the chosen combination of devices is not compatible in view of their original intended use, the system or procedure pack shall be treated as a device in its own right and as such be subjected to the relevant procedure pursuant to Article 11.*

3. Any natural or legal person who sterilizes, for the purpose of placing on the market, systems or procedure packs referred to in paragraph 2 or other CE-marked medical devices designed by their manufacturers to be sterilized before use, shall, at his choice, follow one of the procedures referred to in Annex II or V. The application of the above mentioned Annexes and the intervention of the notified body are limited to the aspects of the procedure relating to the obtaining of sterility until the sterile package is opened or damaged. The person shall draw up a declaration stating that sterilization has been carried out in accordance with the manufacturer's instructions.

4. The products referred to in paragraphs 2 and 3 themselves shall not bear an additional CE marking. They shall be accompanied by the information referred to in point 13 of Annex I which includes, where appropriate, the information supplied by the manufacturers of the devices which have been put together. The declarations referred to in paragraphs 2 and 3 shall be kept at the disposal of the competent authorities for a period of five years.

What You Need to Know

As Dr. D stated in the introduction for this chapter, declarations and compliance

to Annex II and Annex V is everything when complying with Article 12. For those readers that live and breathe the MDD, on a daily basis, the concept of signed declarations is considered routine. However, systems and procedure packs are really in a unique niche and that is why Article 12 is so important. Systems and procedure packs are scenarios where it is possible to have devices from multiple manufacturers and multiple notified bodies placed together to form a singular operating unit or device. For example, an RF Ablation System may have the RF generator from one device manufacturer, a foot-switch and an interface box from another. Somehow, all of this information needs to be collected and retained; henceforth, Article 12. That being said, device manufacturers need to know that there are critical steps associated with this Article.

The first thing device manufacturers need to know and understand is what information is deemed required in the declarations. For systems and procedure packs, there are three salient requirements.

1. The manufacturer tasked with system or procedure pack creation/integration must ensure all of the devices work together, in accordance with their manufacturing instructions. Ensure a validation, incorporating all components (as applicable) has been performed.

2. The packaged systems or procedure packs must include relevant manufacturer instructions.

3. The entire system or procedure pack must meet all of the applicable controls and inspections identified by the manufacturer assembling the systems and packs for resale. If devices incorporated as part of the system or procedure pack are not CE marked, or the packaged compilation of devices <u>are not compatible</u>, in regards to their original intended use, the Article 11 of the MDD is invoked as the governing

requirement for the device.

As expected, sterilization matters. What, device manufacturers have to sterilize procedure packs Dr. D? Not only does sterilization count, in the eyes of the Competent Authorities and the notified bodies, the sterilization facility better have a quality system compliant with Annex II or V of the Directive. How is compliance achieved? The doctor is a big proponent of EN ISO 13485:2003. That said, the only sure-fire way to ensure a sterilizer is compliant with the Directive and EN ISO 13485, is to ask for a copy of their valid certificates, issued by a recognized notified body.

Finally, ensure all of the declarations and applicable certificates are retained for all of the devices included in a system or a procedure pack. Having a strong purchasing and supplier management system in place will facilitate the appropriate controls. In fact, Dr. D strongly recommends having supplier agreements in place for all procured devices.

What You Need to Do

As a device manufacturer, you need to understand the context of Article 12 and ensure systems and procedure packs are handled accordingly. In assembling systems and procedure packs, device manufacturers routinely handle devices with multiple CE marks. One watch out pertains to the presence of a CE Mark. Ensure the CE marks from other device manufactures are not obliterated as part of the packaging or lost in the documentation. Capturing the devices in the actual labeling of the system or procedure pack is extremely important. As for the sterilizer, employing one that has been approved by a recognized notified body, i.e., TUV-R, BSI, TUV-SUD, DEKRA, etc. (no Dr. D is not a paid spokesperson for these organizations) is mission critical. Why? Not wanting to state the obvious but obliged to do so, selecting a sterilization facility that has been approved by a recognized notified body, ensures compliance to EN ISO 13485 and the MDD has been achieved. Finally, ensure all of the declarations, for each of the devices associated with a system or procedure pack, are retained for at least 5-years. It is a requirement that these declarations be at the disposal of the Competent Authorities for at least 5-years.

Takeaways

In regards to this chapter's takeaways, Dr. D will leave you with five; and yes in reading them it will appear that the doctor is sounding like the proverbial broken record.

Number one – device manufacturers need to do their homework when assembling systems or procedure packs. It is incumbent upon the manufacturer to ensure that: (a) the appropriate approvals are in place for each device; (b) the devices work together as advertised; and (c) appropriate instructions are available.

Number two – only work with a sterilizer that has been approved by a recognized notified body.

Number three – ensure each of the devices have a CE mark and the appropriate approvals in place. It will make your life much easier.

Number four - make sure the labeling for systems and procedure packs contain correct references to the devices included.

Number five – documentation is important. Ensure declarations, for each of the devices, are retained for at least 5-years.

Chapter 14 – *Article 12a*
"Reprocessing of Medical Devices"

Chapter Fourteen – Article 12a

Article 12a, of Council Directive 93/42/EEC, a.k.a., the Medical Device Directive (MDD) delineates the requirements for "Reprocessing of Medical Devices." It is Dr. D's opinion that one of the most frustrating issues facing device manufacturers is the reprocessing of their devices. Why? Can you say designed, tested, approved, and sold as a single-use device? I cannot tell you how many times Dr. D has seen user complaints opened against a specific product only to have the product returned to find out the device was manufactured 5-years ago. Wait just a minute, the shelf-life for the device was 37-months, so why is it now just being used. Well folks, the doctor would like to inform you there are just two possible scenarios. In scenario number one, it is just a horrible example of poor inventory control by the healthcare provider, a.k.a. the end user. In scenario two, the device was reprocessed and the only discernable marking is that of the original device manufacturer. Wait a minute Dr. D this cannot still be happening in this age of regulation, can it? Ladies and gentlemen, trust the doctor when I say, it happens frequently. Before I dive into the crux of this chapter's guidance, let Dr. D leave you with one question. How would you like to have an attending physician use a reprocessed device on you or one of your loved ones when a new device is available? Frankly, it would give me the proverbial "willies" knowing that a device being placed into my body has been used multiple times in other patients. One final point, obviously when employing expensive instruments like endoscopes, reprocessing is a necessity driven by cost. Diagnostic catheters used in the field of Electrophysiology, not so much. Just to ensure Dr. D is perfectly clear, the reprocessing of medical devices is a widely-accepted practice; however, the doctor questions the validity or reprocessing devices clearly marketed as single-use, by the manufacturer.

The MDD – 93/42/EEC

Article 12a – Reprocessing of Medical Devices

The Commission shall, no later than 5 September 2010, submit a report to the European Parliament and to the Council on the issue of the reprocessing of medical devices in the Community. In the light of the findings of this report, the Commission shall submit to the European Parliament and to the Council any additional proposal it may deem appropriate in order to ensure a high level of health protection.

What You Need to Know

You can gather from the doctor's poignant introduction, I am not a big fan of reprocessing of single-use devices. Not only are there product performance and sterility risks, it deflates the potential earnings of the manufacturers that have designed, validated, placed into expensive clinical trials, and suffered through lengthy regulatory approval cycles at great expense. I would like to see regulators abrogate (look-it up) the reprocessing of single-use devices; however, it is highly unlikely that will occur. In fact, Dr. D is a staunch believer that reprocessing facilities should be required to complete clinical trials that are identical to the manufacturer in an effort to prove device safety and efficacy, after reprocessing. Regardless, here is what device manufacturers need to know about Article 12a of the MDD.

The reprocessing of medical devices is a reality faced by device manufacturers. There are organizations dedicated to medical device reprocessors. The Association of Medical Device Reprocessors (AMDR) is an organization dedicated to assisting healthcare facilities in the controlling of their skyrocketing costs within the United States. There is a similar organization in Europe, the European Association of Medical Device

Processing (EAMDR). Now Dr. D is not going to debate the virtues of reprocessing; however, device manufacturers need to know that regulations exist, and in some cases no regulations exist, that regulate the practice. In the EU, the acceptance of reprocessed medical devices is extremely diverse with the decision to allow reprocessing premised on decisions made by individual Member States. According to the EAMDR website, the reprocessing of medical devices is broken down into three categories:

1. Regulated/accepted under high quality standards;
2. Not recommended but performed without quality standards; and
3. No legislation but performed without quality structure.

Dr. D strongly recommends visiting the AMDR and EAMDR websites as they are extremely informative and provide the pros and cons (mostly pros) on the topic of reprocessing. Your notified body can guide you through the trials and tribulations of reprocessing for devices marketed in the EU.

What You Need to Do

Device manufactures need to understand that device reprocessing is becoming more prevalent as the cost of healthcare continues to increase substantially. Reprocessing of devices occurs frequently within the EU. As a device manufacturer, it is important to properly label your devices as single-use, although, that will not stop healthcare providers from reprocessing. Device manufacturers need to continue to lobby regulators and educate healthcare practitioners, to ensure stringent procedures are adhered to in regards to reprocessing. For example, if reprocessing continues to be the wave of the future, rigorous validation and testing needs to occur in support of device reprocessing. As stated previously, Dr. D would have reprocessors repeat clinical trials to ensure reprocessed devices are safe and effective. One final thought, the EAMDR website contains an

example where reprocessing of devices is actually prohibited within the EU. Spain,

although no regulations are in place, believes that prohibiting the practice of reprocessing

is the preferred path.

Takeaways

For this chapter, there is just one takeaway. Simply put, the reprocessing of

medical devices is an acceptable practice within the EU. Healthcare providers pursue the

reprocessing of medical devices as a way of controlling costs. Is the practice of

reprocessing single-use devices safe and effective? I will leave that answer to the device

manufacturers as the responses are probably product specific. Generally speaking,

reprocessors believe the practice is safe, device manufacturers, not so much.

"Single-use devices are designed and tested for single use. Reprocessing cannot change this fact."

Chapter 15 – *Article 13*

"Decisions with Regard to Classification and Derogation Clause"

Chapter Fifteen – Article 13

Article 13, of Council Directive 93/42/EEC, a.k.a., the Medical Device Directive (MDD)

delineates the requirements for "Decisions with Regard to Classification and Derogation

Clause." Dr. D believes that the definition of the word *"derogation"* is in order in support

of this chapter. According to Merriam-Webster's Dictionary, the term derogation means

to derogate (just kidding). Derogation is a transitive verb with the meaning of; *"to cause*

to seem inferior." A few of the synonyms associated with the verb derogate are;

denigrate, diminish, discount, or in simple street lingo, trash-talk. Somehow Dr. D does

not think the Commission had the idea of trash-talking in mind when Article 13 was

penned, but it is an interesting selection of a word. Can you picture a broadcaster, at a

pro-sporting event, announcing; "the players are really derogating with each other today."

Not likely to happen in Dr. D's lifetime. In any case, this chapter's guidance is about

Member States questioning authority. Please do not take the doctor's comment the wrong

way in regards to authority. Dr. D does not believe Member States meet in small

conventicles (look-it up) just irk the Commission.

The MDD – 93/42/EEC

Article 13 – Decisions with Regard to Classification and Derogation Clause

1. A Member State shall submit a duly substantiated request to the Commission and ask it to take the necessary measures in the following situations:

> *(a) that Member State considers that the application of the classification rules set out in Annex IX requires a decision with regard to the classification of a given device or category of devices;*
> *(b) that Member State considers that a given device or family of devices should, by way of derogation from the provisions of Annex IX, be classified in another class;*
> *(c) that Member State considers that the conformity of a device or family of devices should, by way of derogation from Article 11, be established by applying solely one of the given procedures chosen from among those referred to in Article 11;*
> *(d) that Member State considers that a decision is required as to whether a particular product or product group falls within one of the definitions in Article 1(2)(a) to (e). The*

measures referred to in the first subparagraph of this paragraph shall, as appropriate, be adopted in accordance with the procedure referred to in Article 7(2).

2. The Commission shall inform the Member States of the measures taken.

What You Need to Know

As a device manufacturer, what you need to know and understand is that Article 13 provides an avenue for Member States to disagree with the Commission in regard to device classification. Sounds pretty simple right? Not exactly. The Member State must eloquently state their case as to why they disagree with the Commission's classification rules for a specific device or family of devices. Remember, device classification is premised on the rules depicted within Annex IV (a.k.a. Classification Rules) of the Directive. Annex IV consists of 5 pages of text delineating 18-rules. That being said, Dr. D has to believe a classification rule exists for every-single device entered into commerce in the European Union. However, the doctor is a pragmatist; and as device technology continues to evolve, the rules will inevitably need to change.

What You Need to Do

As a device manufacturer, understanding the implications of Article 13 is all that is really necessary. However, if a device manufacturer strongly believes that their device is incorrectly classified, they can work through their notified body and see if a specific Member State is willing to elevate the issue to the Commission. It is the doctor's humble opinion that these types of device classification issues, requiring a Competent Authority to petition the Commission, are rare events indeed.

Takeaways

The only takeaway from this chapter offered by the doctor, is to read the Directive and understand the implications each of the Articles and Annexes have on your organization. Yes, Dr. D knows he continues to sound like a broken-record with the often repeated mantra "read and comply with the regulations." However, understanding the context of device regulations, or in the case of this book, the MDD, is synonymous with sustaining regulatory compliance. Remember DG Rule #1 - Compliance to regulations is not optional; compliance is mandatory and dictated by law.

"Remember, the Notified Bodies work for you; however, they receive their power from the Competent Authorities from specific Member States."

Chapter 16 – *Article 14*

"Registration of Persons Responsible for Placing Devices on the Market"

Chapter Sixteen – Article 14

Article 14, of Council Directive 93/42/EEC, a.k.a., the Medical Device Directive (MDD) delineates the requirements for "*Registration of persons responsible for placing devices on the market.*" I wanted to start this chapter's guidance with a quick story. I received an email from a dear friend of mine living in Ireland concerning my use of the MS Word™ spell-check feature. He asked me, "How come Dr. D was changing the spelling for some of the key terms, e.g., authorized versus authorized?" My answer was quite simple; "Some folks need to learn how to spell." His response, "Well Chris, I can teach you if you give me a chance, and a few pints." A few pints actually sounds like a good deal. Moving on, as Dr. D will continue to concatenate (look-it up if you must) chapters of this book on complying with the MDD. The underlying theme of this book will continue to be compliance, compliance, and more compliance. The doctor continues to receive a significant volume of email reminding me that distributing devices into the EU is viewed as somehow being different than entering product into commerce within the United States. My answer is; "no, not really." Just as in the United States and the Quality System Regulation, the MDD is law for 27-Member States (27 as of this book). Failure to comply with the Directive will result in product being blocked from entry into the EU. Can you say; "Please remove our CE Mark immediately?" Since the CE Mark belongs to your notified body, they retain the right to ask for its removal, if compliance issues arise.

The MDD – 93/42/EEC

Article 14 – Registration of persons responsible for placing devices on the market

1. Any manufacturer who, under his own name, places devices on the market in accordance with the procedures referred to in Article 11 (5) and (6) and any other natural or legal person engaged in the activities referred to in Article 12 shall inform the competent authorities of the Member State in which he has his registered place of business of the address of the registered place of business and the description of the devices concerned. For all medical devices of classes IIa, IIb and III, Member States may request to be informed of all data allowing for identification of such devices together with the label and the instructions for use when such devices are put into service within their territory.

2. Where a manufacturer who places a device on the market under his own name does not have a registered place of business in a Member State, he shall designate a single authorized representative in the European Union. For devices referred to in the first subparagraph of paragraph 1, the authorized representative shall inform the competent authority of the Member State in which he has his registered place of business of the details referred to in paragraph 1.

3. The Member States shall on request inform the other Member States and the Commission of the details referred to in the first subparagraph of paragraph 1given by the manufacturer or authorised representative.

What You Need to Know

As a device manufacturer, Article 14 is an extremely important one to understand. Under Article 14, device manufacturers are required to establish a European Authorized (sorry friend - spelled correctly in the U.S.) Representative. The good news is that device manufacturers are not required to have an EU Authorized Rep in each Member State. One will do just fine. Additionally, the EU Authorized Rep should have an accurate list containing the product names, UPNs, etc. of all of the devices entered into commerce within the EU. Furthermore, device manufacturer's need to have a written contract/agreement with their EU Authorized Rep. Although not spelled out directly in Article 14, your notified body will ask to see a current contract/agreement during their annual visit to your facility. Finally, make sure that the address of the EU Authorized Rep makes its way onto the actual product labeling. It is Dr. D's humble opinion; it is a salient requirement equal to that of the CE Mark being placed on the product labeling.

What You Need to Do

Number one - not wanting to state the obvious, but obliged to do so, device manufacturers need to establish a European Authorized Representative Office in a Member State. There are 27 so just pick one. This is not an option. Number two – device manufacturers need to ensure a written contract/agreement is in place with the EU Authorized Rep. This document should clearly delineated the responsibilities for each party within the body of the agreement. Number three – ensure the EU Authorized Rep has an accurate list of devices being sold into the EU. Device manufacturers can perform a quick check for accuracy by comparing the product list residing with the EU Authorized Rep and the list(s) maintained by your notified body or bodies, if you have more than one. Number four – ensure the EU Authorized Rep address makes its way onto the product labeling. It is a legal requirement for product entering into commerce within all 27-Member States.

Takeaways

The takeaway for this chapter is extremely simple and once again, the redundancy results in Dr. D entering the realm of broken-record time. However, understanding Article 14 is vitally important. Device manufacturers need to retain a European Authorized Representative in order to place medical devices into commerce in the EU. There needs to be: (a) a contract with the EU Authorized Rep; (b) an accurate product list on file with the EU Authorized Rep; and (c) the EU Authorized Rep address needs to be on the product labeling.

"Having an EU Authorized Rep is not optional."

Chapter 17 – *Article 14a*

"European Databank"

Chapter Seventeen – Article 14a

Article 14a, of Council Directive 93/42/EEC, a.k.a., the Medical Device Directive

(MDD) delineates the requirements for "*European Databank*." This chapter, simply put,

relates to the European Union (EU) and their need to develop a standardized format for

data collection associated with medical devices; and a receptacle for collecting

voluminous amounts of data. Simply collecting data and housing it in a vitrine (look-it-

up) just for the sake of having it, makes zero sense. Just an FYI from Dr. D, according to

the Directive, the provisions of Article 14a must be incorporated by 5 September 2012

with a review by the Commission the following month. Getting 27-Member States to

agree on data format and the appropriate platform for the databank must have been an

interesting endeavor indeed. That being said, the European Databank on Medical Devices

(EUDAMED) is currently live (beta-site) with a handful of Member States using it on a

voluntary basis. Dr. D strongly suggests checking out the Website (listed under

references at the end of the book); however, the site's data access is restricted and not

available to the general public. The purpose of EUDAMED is to "strengthen market

surveillance and transparency" for medical devices in the EU. The databank provides

real-time information to the Competent Authorities from each Member State.

The MDD – 93/42/EEC

Article 14a – European Databank

1. Regulatory data in accordance with this Directive shall be stored in a European database accessible to the competent authorities to enable them to carry out their tasks relating to this Directive on a well- informed basis. The databank shall contain the following:

> *(a) data relating to registration of manufacturers and authorized representatives and devices in accordance with Article 14 excluding data related to custom-made devices;*

(b) data relating to certificates issued, modified, supplemented, suspended, withdrawn or refused according to the procedures, as laid down in Annexes II to VII;

(c) data obtained in accordance with the vigilance procedure as defined in Article 10;

(d) data relating to clinical investigations referred to in Article 15.

2. Data shall be forwarded in a standardized format.

3. The measures necessary for the implementation of paragraphs 1 and 2 of this Article, in particular paragraph 1(d), shall be adopted in accordance with the regulatory procedure referred to in Article 7(2).

4. The provisions of this Article shall be implemented no later than 5 September 2012. The Commission shall, no later than 11 October 2012, evaluate the operational functioning and the added value of the databank. On the basis of this evaluation, the Commission shall, if appropriate, present proposals to the European Parliament and the Councilor present draft measures in accordance with paragraph 3.

What You Need to Know

As a device manufacturer, Article 14a is nothing more than an FYI. The Article has several salient points you should be familiar with, including the employment of the Global Medical Device Nomenclature (GMDN) code for your devices. The salient requirement for Article 14a is that a regulatory database shall be developed. As Dr. D stated in the opening paragraph, this has successfully occurred under the name of EUDAMED, with a working beta-site available for use by the Competent Authorities. As a minimum, the databank shall contain:

- Manufacturer's registration data;

- European Authorized Representative data;

- Device registration data (excluding custom-made devices);

- Certification Data (issued, modified, supplemented, suspended, withdrawn and/or refused);

- Data collected in support of vigilance procedures; and

- Data for clinical investigations.

The next requirement of Article 14a is that the format for data will need to be standardized. Obviously, for the databank concept to work efficiently, the data must be organized in a format that supports the databank's architecture. Standardization of the data format is the only real plausible approach. Employment of the GMDN becomes an important input for EUDAMED in support of standardization.

Remember, the key dates associated with the implementation of Article 14a are September 5, 2012 and October 11, 2012. The first date being the completion of implementation activities (looks like an early success); and the second date, the evaluation of the databank by the Commission. From Dr. D's perspective, I guess the Commission felt compelled to ensure the databank was fully operational before 12/21/12, the official end of the Mayan Calendar.

What You Need to Do

As the doctor stated earlier, there is no immediate impact for device manufacturers other than ensuring your products have the correct GMDN associated with them. However, Dr. D is a gambling man. That being said, I bet that someday there will be changes in the approach notified bodies take to manage their certificates, including the look and content. It would make sense to have a standardized format for certificates; and I suspect this will be coming. Then again, Dr. D could be wrong. Regardless, the probability for standardization of certificates can be found somewhere between pipedream and conjecture on the part of Dr. D.

Takeaways

For this Chapter, the only takeaway for device manufacturers is that the EU continues with their pursuit of standardization in supporting the establishment of effective data management, with the development and launching of EUDAMED, their new databank. Dr. D loves standardization because when it is pursued, with some intelligence, the end result is the creation of tools that make device manufacturer's lives a bit easier. The doctor does strongly recommend a review of products to ensure devices are properly assigned the correct GMDN. Your notified body can help with this task. On the flip side of the argument, the EU will be better able to manage the regulatory aspect of medical devices. Problem devices and device manufacturers will be able to be identified quickly and the appropriate regulatory action pursued.

"EUDAMED is on the horizon and should help greatly with the management of data within the EU."

Chapter 18 – *Article 14b*

"Particular Health Monitoring Measures"

Chapter Eighteen – Article 14b

Article 14b, of Council Directive 93/42/EEC, a.k.a., the Medical Device Directive

(MDD) delineates the requirements for *"Particular Health Monitoring Measures."* Can

you say market withdraw? The axiomatic (look-it-up) concept of withdrawing product

from the European market equates to just one simple 6-letter word, "RECALL." Article

14b, of the Directive, is all about Member States having the power to force products or

groups of products off the market in support of preserving public health. Additionally,

Article 14b gives Member States the power to block, restrict or subject to additional

requirements, devices or groups of devices. Once a Member State had taken appropriate

action to protect public health and safety within their own borders, the Member State

must notify the Commission and other Member States in regards to action taken. The

onus of making a decision is then placed squarely on the shoulders of the Commission.

The Commission will consult with Member States and interested parties, e.g., device

manufacturer(s) and decide if the action pursued by the Member State is justified.

Furthermore, when deemed necessary and appropriate, additional regulatory action can

be pursued up to and including the amending of non-essential Directive elements

influencing market withdraw and/or prohibiting introduction of products, so products can

eventually enter the European Market. Finally, when all else fails the Commission has the

authority to invoke Article 7(4), a.k.a. the urgency procedure.

The MDD – 93/42/EEC

Article 14b – Particular Health Monitoring Measures

Where a Member State considers, in relation to a given product or group of products,
that, in order to ensure protection of health and safety and/or to ensure that public health
requirements are observed, such products should be withdrawn from the market, or their

placing on the market and putting into service should be prohibited, restricted or subjected to particular requirements, it may take any necessary and justified transitional measures. The Member State shall then inform the Commission and all other Member States, giving the reasons for its decision. The Commission shall, whenever possible, consult the interested Parties and the Member States. The Commission shall adopt its opinion, indicating whether the national measures are justified or not. The Commission shall inform all the Member States and the consulted interested Parties thereof. When appropriate, the necessary measures designed to amend nonessential elements of this Directive, relating to withdrawal from the market, prohibition of placing on the market and putting into service of a certain product or group of products or to restrictions or introduction of particular requirements in order for such products to be put on the market, shall be adopted in accordance with the regulatory procedure with scrutiny referred to in Article 7(3). On imperative grounds of urgency, the Commission may use the urgency procedure referred to in Article 7(4).

What You Need to Know

Hopefully, as a device manufacturer, you will never face the dilemma of dealing with Article 14b. However, the device manufacturing industry is far from utopic; and that is why copious amounts of regulations exist. That being said, just as in death and taxes, it is inevitable device manufacturers will suffer through a forced product withdraw or prohibition of market entry of devices into the EU. On a positive note, that is why device manufacturers retain and pay dearly, their notified bodies. A competent notified body will help device manufactures navigate the sometimes turbulent waters of the European device market. As with all regulations arising from participation in multiple markets, the device manufacturer should have a thorough grasp and understanding of the applicable regulations. In the support of this chapter's guidance, Dr. D strongly suggests understanding the content of Article 14b and the potential impact the Article has on your business. Remember, forced-market withdraws, or a complete blockage of your devices from entering a Member State(s) equates to an interruption in the revenue stream. Simply stated, "Not making euros is a bad thing." Yes, the doctor sounds like a capitalist; however, Dr. D is also a pragmatist and a realist.

What You Need to Do

Device manufacturers need to work closely with their notified bodies to ensure their business is never placed at risk with the Competent Authorities in the EU. Article 14b is very real in regards to Member States taking the appropriate action to protect public safety and health. Dr. D always recommends that device manufacturers ensure compliance to device essential requirements is always established. This commences with a robust design and development process and continues through validation testing. A robust design should result in manufactured medical devices that are safe and effective. If a device is safe and effective, then Article 14b of the Directive will never be an issue for device manufacturers.

Takeaways

Device manufacturers should never attempt to ensconce (look-it-up) device problems in an effort to circumvent Article 14b. In fact, the EU is becoming much smarter in regards to collecting device data, especially for problem devices. Going back to the previous chapter, the European Databank (EUDAMED) will be fully functional in 2012. That being said, there are two takeaways from this chapter. One – a robust design and development process will lead to medical devices that are safe and effective. Two – devices that are safe and effective; and meet their essential requirements, seldom if ever will run afoul of Article 14b of the MDD. In closing, use your notified body for guidance. They make a substantial amount of coin from their customers (you), so device manufacturers should ensure they get their money's worth.

"Simple fact, a forced market withdraw will result in the interruption of revenue."

Chapter 19 – *Article 15*

"Clinical Investigation"

Chapter Nineteen – Article 15

Article 15, of Council Directive 93/42/EEC, a.k.a., the Medical Device Directive (MDD) delineates the requirements for "*Clinical investigation.*" Basically, Article 15 provides the guidelines for device manufacturers that have product or are planning to introduce product, into a European Union (EU) Member State, for the purpose of conducting a clinical investigation. Long gone are the days when device manufacturers had a simple clinical protocol in their hands and a box full of devices to verify product safety and efficacy. In days of old, device manufactures typically pursued a terpsichorean (look-it-up) approach to clinical trials effectively dancing around regulations that were often vague. Revisions to the MDD now clarify and solidify regulatory requirements for device manufacturers wishing to pursue clinical investigations within the EU. Failure to comply with Article 15 of the Directive will result in device manufacturers failing to obtain approval to pursue clinical investigations within the EU. In today's increasingly complex medical device market, not performing a clinical investigation will result in device manufacturers being shutout of the European market. In fact, without data collected as a result of a well-run clinical investigation, Dr. D can safely hypothesize; "Device manufacturers will be shutout of most markets without supporting clinical data."

The MDD – 93/42/EEC

Article 15 – Clinical Investigation

1. In the case of devices intended for clinical investigations, the manufacturer or the authorized representative, established in the Community, shall follow the procedure referred to in Annex VIII and notify the competent authorities of the Member States in which the investigations are to be conducted by means of the statement mentioned in Section 2.2 of Annex VIII.

2. In the case of devices falling within Class III and implantable and long-term invasive devices falling within Class IIa or IIb, the manufacturer may commence the relevant clinical investigation at the end of a period of 60 days after notification, unless the competent authorities have notified him within that period of a decision to the contrary based on considerations of public health or public policy. Member States may however authorize manufacturers to commence the relevant clinical investigations before the expiry of the period of 60 days, insofar as the relevant ethics committee has issued a favorable opinion on the program of investigation in question, including its review of the clinical investigation plan.

3. In the case of devices other than those referred to in paragraph 2, Member States may authorize manufacturers to commence clinical investigations immediately after the date of notification, provided that the ethics committee concerned has issued a favorable opinion on the program of investigation in question including its review of the clinical investigation plan.

4. The authorization referred to in paragraph 2 second subparagraph and paragraph 3, maybe made subject to authorization from the competent authority

5. The clinical investigations must be conducted in accordance with the provisions of Annex X. The measures designed to amend nonessential elements of this Directive, inter alia by supplementing it, relating to the provisions on clinical investigation in Annex X shall be adopted in accordance with the regulatory procedure with scrutiny referred to in Article 7(3).

6. The Member States shall, if necessary, take the appropriate steps to ensure public health and public policy. Where a clinical investigation is refused or halted by a Member State, that Member State shall communicate its decision and the grounds therefor to all Member States and the Commission. Where a Member State has called for a significant modification or temporary interruption of a clinical investigation, that Member State shall inform the Member States concerned about its actions and the grounds for the actions taken.

7. The manufacturer or his authorized representative shall notify the competent authorities of the Member States concerned of the end of the clinical investigation, with a justification in case of early termination. In the case of early termination of the clinical investigation on safety grounds this notification shall be communicated to all Member States and the Commission. The manufacturer or his authorized representative shall keep the report referred to in Section 2.3.7 of Annex X at the disposal of the competent authorities.

8. The provisions of paragraphs 1 and 2 do not apply where the clinical investigations are conducted using devices which are authorized in accordance with Article 11 to bear the CE marking unless the aim of these investigations is to use the devices for a purpose other than that referred to in the relevant conformity assessment procedure. The relevant provisions of Annex X remain applicable.

What You Need to Know

The first responsibility for device manufacturers, associated with introducing devices for clinical evaluation into a Member State, is the notification made to the Competent Authority responsible for the Member State, where the clinical investigation will be performed. If multiple Member States are to be included in the clinical investigation, then multiple Competent Authorities will need to be notified. Simply stated, "That is the law." Notification can also be made through the device manufacturer's European Authorized Representative, for device manufacturers not having a manufacturing presence within the EU.

Dr. D knows that device manufacturers love to play the waiting game in regards to regulatory requirements. That being said, there is a 60-day notification period associated with performing clinical investigations. This 60-day period applies to Class III devices, implantable devices, Class IIb devices that can be categorizes as long-term invasive, and Class IIa devices that can be categorized as long-term invasive. The doctor is not always the purveyor of bad news, contrary to popular belief, so Dr. D will commence with the good news first. If a review by the applicable ethics committee, within a Member State(s), views the proposed clinical investigation and the protocol favorably, they can approve the investigation to commence in under 60-days. Do you remember the old saying, "no news is good news?" If at the end of 60-days, if Competent Authorities have not provided a negative opinion, the clinical investigation can commence at the end of the 60-day notification period. Now for the bad news, the Competent Authorities are charged with protecting the public health of the constituents of their Member States; and they have the right to just say _**NO**_, if they have concerns over the proposed clinical investigation and the written protocol.

Additionally, for lower-risk devices, not mentioned in the doctor's previous paragraph, manufacturers can commence with their investigations immediately after notification is made, providing the appropriate ethics committee has ruled favorably in regards to the proposed clinical investigation and the protocol. Once approval is received, the device manufacturer can commence with executing the clinical investigation. A salient point that device manufacturers should never overlook is the requirement to ensure the clinical investigation is conducted in accordance with Annex X of the Directive. Annex X of the MDD delineates the requirements for performing *"**Clinical Evaluations**."*

One point the doctor feels compelled to make and will continue to do so over and over again; is that the Competent Authorities are charged with protecting public health for their Member State. Yes Dr. D, broken-record time, and I do get it! That being said, if a Member State refuses a clinical investigation or makes a decision to halt a clinical investigation (they have the legal right); the Member State making the decision must share the decision with all Member States and the Commission. Additionally, if a Member State believes the clinical investigation requires modification, this too must be shared with other Member States participating in the clinical investigation. The notification must include the grounds the decision for modification was premised on, and the recommended modifications to the clinical investigation.

Conversely, the device manufacturer or the manufacturer's Authorized Rep, is tasked with notifying the Competent Authorities for each Member State participating in the clinical investigation, upon conclusion of the investigation. If the clinical investigation is ended earlier than the planned schedule, a written rationale is required delineating the reason(s) behind the early termination. If the clinical investigation is terminated for safety reasons, the reasons must be communicated to all Member States and the Commission. One watch out for device manufacturers is to ensure data management associated with the clinical investigation and the subsequent reports should be managed in accordance with Annex X of the Directive. Why? Because the Competent Authorities may ask for this information, so it needs to be, *"at their disposal."*

One final point, when devices are CE Marked and are authorized for entry and use within the EU, in accordance with Article 11 of the Directive, paragraph 1 and 2 of Article 15 do not apply, unless the proposed clinical investigation is for a new intended use, for which the CE Marked device is not currently approved. Regardless, Annex X of the Directive will still remain as a relevant compliance requirement.

What You Need to Do

Device manufacturers need to ensure approval is received from the Competent Authority for each Member State for which a clinical investigation will be performed. If the device manufacturer is located outside of the European Economic Community (EEC), the correct conduit for this notification will be their Authorized Rep. Your notified body can guide you through the process. It is extremely important that device manufacturers understand that there is a 60-day review period during which the Competent Authorities and ethics committees, for each Member State, will review the proposed clinical investigation and protocol. Approval can occur in less than the mandated 60-day period; however, Dr. D's experience is that this early approval is a rare event.

Once the clinical investigation commences, Member States have the right to suspend or order modifications to clinical investigations if a potential risk to public health is discovered. Conversely, device manufactures have the right to suspend an investigation for this very same reason. What device manufacturers need to do is to ensure all of the appropriate notifications are made when: (a) a decision is made to end a clinical investigation early; (b) suspend or end a clinical investigation due to a concern over the potential risk to public health; or (c) when the clinical investigation reaches conclusion, as documented within the approved protocol.

It is extremely important, in fact, it should be considered mission critical, that clinical investigations be executed in accordance with Annex X of the Directive (yes – broken record time again but this is important). Remember, the Competent Authorities have the legal right to access the data collected during the clinical investigation. Their expectation is that device manufacturers will comply with all of the provisions delineated within Annex X. Failure to comply and the Competent Authorities can unleash an onslaught of regulatory pain for device manufacturers. This is especially true for clinical investigations that harm participants.

Takeaways

Clinical investigations are a mandated requirement for device manufacturer's intent on entering new devices into the EU. Gone are the days when loosely-run clinical investigations/trials, a competitor's trial, or limited-use data was accepted as part of the application process. Device manufacturers are required to comply with Article 15 for new clinical investigations. That being said, the takeaways for this chapter are:

1. Approval is required from each Member State participating in the proposed clinical investigation;

2. There is a mandatory 60-day review period;

3. Member States can say no to a proposed clinical investigation;

4. Member States can suspend or request modifications to a clinical investigation;

5. Device manufacturers can suspend or end a clinical investigation early;

6. Device manufacturers need to ensure the appropriate notifications are made when they decide to suspend or end a clinical investigation early;

7. Once the clinical investigation protocol has been executed and the investigation comes to its planned ending, device manufacturers must notify Member States; and

8. All clinical investigations must be executing in accordance with the provisions delineated with Annex X of the Directive.

"Under changes incorporated into revisions of the MDD made in 2010, clinical investigations and assessments are not longer optional."

Chapter 20 – *Article 16*
"Notified Bodies"

Chapter Twenty – Article 16

Article 16, of Council Directive 93/42/EEC, a.k.a., the Medical Device Directive (MDD) delineates the requirements for *"Notified Bodies."* For device manufacturers, the path to placing product into commerce within the European Union (EU) is through the notified bodies. In fact, the notified body, selected by a device manufacturer, will become a long-term partner, not unlike a marriage. That being said, it is important to select a notified body an organization will be comfortable working with as a valued and trusted partner. One key concept to remember is that although the notified bodies are tasked with the review and approval of product applications for device manufacturers, including the design dossiers and technical files, they actual work for the manufacturer. The device manufacturer contracts with and pays the notified body for their services. Just wait until the device manufacturer receiving the invoices. Another salient point needing to be made is that the notified body owns the CE Mark containing their registration number. For example, if a device manufacturer decided to choose TUV-R as their notified body, once product was approved for sale into the EU, the CE Mark containing the registration number 0197 would be affixed to all products entering into commerce within the EU. Simply put, no CE Mark equates to no European device sales. In fact, good luck with trying to ship product into one of the 27-Member States. One final note, it is Dr. D's personal opinion, a few notified bodies believe that they are holier than thou; however, device manufacturers should never feel obliged to pay obeisance (look-it up) to these regulatory bodies because at the end of the day, they are on your payroll, so choose wisely.

The MDD – 93/42/EEC

Article 16 – Notified Bodies

1. The Member States shall notify the Commission and other Member States of the bodies which they have designated for carrying out the tasks pertaining to the procedures referred to in Article 11 and the specific tasks for which the bodies have been designated. The Commission shall assign identification numbers to these bodies, here in after referred to as 'notified bodies'. The Commission shall publish a list of the notified bodies, together with the identification numbers it has allocated to them and the tasks for which they have been notified, in the Official Journal of the European Communities. It shall ensure that the list is kept up to date.

2. Member States shall apply the criteria set out in Annex XI for the designation of bodies. Bodies that meet the criteria laid down in the national standards which transpose the relevant harmonized standards shall be presumed to meet the relevant criteria. When appropriate in the light of technical progress, the detailed measures necessary to ensure a consistent application of the criteria set out in Annex XI for the designation of bodies by the Member States shall be adopted in accordance with the regulatory procedure referred to in Article 7(2).

3. A Member State that has notified a body shall withdraw that notification if it finds that the body no longer meets the criteria referred to in paragraph 2. It shall immediately inform the other Member States and the Commission thereof.

4. The notified body and the manufacturer, or his authorized representative shall lay down, by common accord, the time limits for completion of the assessment and verification operations referred to in Annexes II to VI.

5. The notified body shall inform its competent authority about all certificates issued, modified, supplemented, suspended, withdrawn or refused and the other notified bodies within the scope of this Directive about certificates suspended, withdrawn or refused and, on request, about certificates issued. The notified body shall also make available, on request, all additional relevant information.

6. Where a notified body finds that pertinent requirements of this Directive have not been met or are no longer met by the manufacturer or where a certificate should not have been issued, it shall, taking account of the principle of proportionality, suspend or withdraw the certificate issued or place any restrictions on it unless compliance with such requirements is ensured by the implementation of appropriate corrective measures by the manufacturer. In the case of suspension or withdrawal of the certificate or of any restriction placed on it or in cases where an intervention of the competent authority may become necessary, the notified body shall inform its competent authority thereof. The Member State shall inform the other Member States and the Commission.

7. The notified body shall, on request, supply all relevant information and documents including budgetary documents, required to enable the Member State to verify compliance with Annex XI requirements.

What You Need to Know

The first thing device manufacturers need to know is that notified bodies just do not come into being. There is no such thing as a regulatory immaculate conception. The notified bodies are chartered by the Member States from which they operate. For example, NSAI operates out of Ireland and the Irish Competent Authority is tasked with their oversight and their ongoing authority to perform approved regulatory tasks. Additionally, Member States must notify the Commission, providing the Commission with the names of approved notified bodies. Upon notification, the Commission is charged with issuing the registration number; henceforth, the birth of the notified body. This birth is then recorded in the Official Journal. Each notified body will have their own unique registration number.

The next step is for Member States to invoke Annex XI (Criterion to be met for the Designation of Notified Bodies) in regards to ensuring notified bodies operating within their jurisdiction remain in compliance with the MDD. Not unlike the notified bodies and their ability to make a device manufacturer's life miserable during an annual audit, the Competent Authorities can do the same to notified bodies. At the end of the day, the message within the EU is now and continues to be compliance, compliance, and more compliance. Yes, the doctor knows that he continues to sound like a broken record when he climbs onto his soapbox to preach compliance.

A salient point to remember is that a Member State has the legal authority to withdraw the certification of a notified body that fails to sustain ongoing compliance with the Directive. The message being sent is clear; Member States and the Commission are looking for **compliance with the Directive** at all levels (yes – broken record).

Once commissioned, the notified body must establish and convey to the device manufacturer or the manufacturer's European Authorized Representative, the frequency and time limits established for assessments/activities in which ongoing operations of device manufacturers are assessed for compliance with Annex II through Annex VI. Device manufacturers can expect these friendly visits at least once per year. Guess what? Device manufacturers also get to pay for this annual abuse. Why - because the notified bodies work for you; and device manufacturers will pay dearly for this work. I know, broken-record time again, but these points are important.

Another mission-critical point device manufacturers need to comprehend is that their notified body has the legal right to refuse the issuance of a certificate, revoke a certificate, suspend a certificate, or withdraw a certificate issued to a device manufacturer. Although a rare event indeed, a suspended or withdrawn certificate can result in the temporary and potentially long-term interruption of a revenue stream. No product sales, results in no money coming into the corporate coffers. Ouch! If such action is pursued by the notified body, they are tasked with notifying the Competent Authority. Ouch, Ouch!

Additionally, if a notified body is able to ascertain that a device manufacturer has failed to meet the requirements delineated within the Directive or that a certificate should never have been issued; they are required to pursue an appropriate course of action, ASAP! The doctor would love to be the proverbial "fly-on-the-wall" when a notified body has the discussion with their Competent Authority, explaining how the issuance of a certificate was a mistake. Big Ouch! Is it appropriate to use the phrase, "my bad" in Europe? As a manufacturer, losing a certificate is not the end of the world. The notified body will ask that corrective action be taken to resolve the compliance issues. Once the notified body believes a device manufacturer has adequately corrected the objectionable conditions, the certification can be reissued. It should be noted, the Competent Authority

115

retains the legal right to intervene when certification issues arise. Regardless, when certification issues arise, the notified body notifies the Competent Authority, the Competent Authority notifies the Member State, and the Member State notifies other Member States, and ultimately the Commission. Before long, the entire continent of Europe is aware that a device manufacturer's certificate(s) have been pulled. Really Big Ouch!

Finally, upon request, notified bodies are required to provide documentation and other information in support of claiming ongoing compliance, with Annex XI, to the appropriate Member State. This information will be employed by the Member State to validate the ongoing compliance with the Directive by notified bodies.

What You Need to Do

First and foremost, device manufacturers need to strive to sustain an ongoing state of compliance with the Directive (yes – broken record time). One major deviation received during an annual surveillance audit is all it takes to place a certificate(s) in jeopardy. If notified bodies are executing their duties diligently and according to the Directive, and the working relationship with the device manufacturer is a close and nurturing one, there should never be any surprises.

As a device manufacturer, you should be aware that not all notified bodies are created equal. It is the strong opinion of Dr. D; some notified bodies are clearly better than others. Organizations such as TUV-R, TUV-SUD, BSI, NSAI, and DEKRA (no the doctor is not a paid spokesperson for these organizations) are recognized as some of the industry leaders.

Once a device application is approved, device manufacturers need to ensure all product labeling contains reference to the appropriate CE Mark. An example I presented a few paragraphs ago made reference to CE 0197 (TUV-R). As a minimum, this mark needs to be affixed to the outermost carton / box, pouch, DFU, etc. It is a legal requirement. Additionally, Dr. D recommends a review of EN 980:2008 to ensure all symbols placed onto the label are correct. Another point the doctor must emphatically make is that, "The notified bodies give and the notified bodies can take away," in regards to certificates. Remember, the CE Mark and registration number belongs to them. Device manufacturers are just renting the CE Mark, so to speak.

Finally, device manufacturers need to clearly understand the relationship between the notified body, Competent Authority, Member State, and the Commission. If devices are deemed not to be safe and effective within the EU, the Competent Authority can also authorized the suspension or withdrawing of a device manufacturer's certificate.

Takeaways

For this chapter, Dr. D will keep it simple. There are five salient takeaways that device manufacturers need to understand.

- The notified body issues certification and the notified body can take away the certification.

- The CE Mark of registration is assigned by the Commission and belongs to the notified body.

- Once a device manufacturer receive certification they, are responsible for ensuring the CE Mark is applied to product appropriately.

- If a certificate is withdrawn, device manufacturers must remove the CE Mark of conformity; no argument or discussion is required because that is the law.

- Competent Authorities also retain the authority to force the suspension or revocation of a certificate, if devices entering into commerce in the EU are found not to be safe and effective.

"Remember the relationship with the Notified Body is not unlike a marriage!"

Chapter 21 – *Article 17 "CE Marking"*

Chapter Twenty-one – Article 17

Article 17, of Council Directive 93/42/EEC, a.k.a., the Medical Device Directive (MDD) delineates the requirements for "*CE Marking*." Dr. D would like to begin this chapter with one of my broken-record comments; "No CE Marking equates to no revenue stream coming from the European Union (EU)." Why? Because having the CE Marking of conformity, visible and legible, on the outermost packaging, is a fundamental requirement. In the previous chapter, the doctor discussed notified bodies and their owning of a specific registration number associated with the CE Marking. If you have not read the previous chapter, Dr. D recommends doing so before continuing with this chapter. Remember the path to conformity is premised on the classification of the device and the evidence of compliance with essential requirements delineated within the Directive. The notified body, which medical device companies pay so handsomely to help facilitate the entry of their devices into the EU, will assist in the device application and perform the actual review of the technical file or design dossier before issuing certification. The device manufacturer **cannot affix** the CE Marking, until certification is issued. To do so, would be a violation of the Directive and result in the immediate forced withdraw of non-approved product from the EU, including the public flogging of an organization's Chief Jailable Officer (CJO). Yes, Dr. D is just kidding about the public flogging. Besides, no device manufacturer wants to endear themselves with the Competent Authorities by partaking in such a bold and brazen act. The Competent Authorities and their philippic (look-it up) aimed directly at the offending device manufacturer would be extremely painful in its own right. Ouch!

The MDD – 93/42/EEC

Article 17 – CE Marking

1. Devices, other than devices which are custom-made or intended for clinical investigations, considered to meet the essential requirements referred to in Article 3 must bear the CE marking of conformity when they are placed on the market.

2. The CE marking of conformity, as shown in Annex XII, must appear in a visible, legible and indelible form on the device or its sterile pack, where practicable and appropriate, and on the instructions for use. Where applicable, the CE marking must also appear on the sales packaging. It shall be accompanied by the identification number of the notified body responsible for implementation of the procedures set out in Annexes II, IV, V and VI.

3. It is prohibited to affix marks or inscriptions which are likely to mislead third parties with regard to the meaning or the graphics of the CE marking. Any other mark maybe affixed to the device, to the packaging or to the instruction leaflet accompanying the device provided that the visibility and legibility of the CE marking is not thereby reduced.

What You Need to Know

The first thing device manufacturers need to know and understand is that affixing of the CE Marking is premised on a device meeting essential requirements. The notified body will determine if conformity has been achieved and issue certification if appropriate. Broken-record time again, "then and only then will a device manufacture legally be able to affix the CE Mark." This is an extremely important point to takeaway form this chapter.

Additionally, there are certain dimensional requirements in regards to the CE Marking. Annex XII delineates: *"The CE conformity marking shall consist of the initials 'CE' taking the following form: If the marking is reduced or enlarged the proportions given in the above graduated drawing must be respected. The various components of the CE marking must have substantially the same vertical dimension, which may not be less than 5 mm. This minimum dimension maybe waived for small-scale devices."* The notified body can help with the artwork for their CE Marking and their identification number e.g., CE0197, belonging to TUV-R. Regardless, the point that should be understood is; if the CE Marking requires resizing due to space restrictions or package dimensions, the proportions must remain constant.

Furthermore, the Directive prohibits device manufacturers from altering the CE Marking or adding additional markings, inscriptions, or anything else that would potentially confuse or intentionally mislead third parties (a.k.a., the customer). The safe rule of thumb is to ensure the CE Marking is clearly visible and legible, period!

What You Need to Do

Simply stated, "Device manufacturers should never affix a CE Mark to their product until certification is received from their notified body." Dr. D strongly recommends ensuring all of the product labeling, including symbols are clear, concise, and in compliance with EN 980. A watch out - if your organization has multiple notified bodies, make sure the correct CE Marking, containing the correct notified body registration number is affixed to correct product. No the doctor is not off his rocker. In fact, Dr. D has experienced the pain associated with the affixing of the incorrect CE Mark, on the wrong product, first hand. Trust the doctor when I say, the recall and subsequent rework can be costly; including the explanation issued to multiple notified bodies explaining how such an error occurred in the first place. Yes, size matters, when talking about the dimensions associated with the CE Marking. Use Annex XII of the Directive as guidance. The key is to ensure that if resizing occurs, the elements of the CE Marking remain in proportion to each other.

Takeaways

For this chapter, there are three concepts to take away from this guidance.

1. Devices entering into commerce within the EU, unless identified as custom-made

or for a clinical investigation, require a CE Marking that indicates conformity to its essential requirements. A device manufacturer cannot affix the CE Marking until certification is issued by their notified body.

2. The CE Marking must be visible and legible. Annex XII delineates the dimensional requirements of the CE Marking.

3. The CE Marking cannot be altered, changed, improved upon, hidden, obstructed, defaced, or augmented in a manner that would result in the misleading of a third party. Remember, the notified bodies like their CE Marks, as is, and see no need for device manufacturers to improve upon this small master piece.

"No CE Marking equates to no revenue stream coming from the European Union (EU)."

Chapter 22 – *Article 18*
"Wrongly Affixed CE Marking"

Chapter Twenty-two – Article 18

Article 18 of Council Directive 93/42/EEC, a.k.a., the Medical Device Directive (MDD) delineates the requirements for *"Wrongly Affixed CE Marking."* This chapter is all about the mark, the whole mark, and nothing but the mark. As Dr. D stated in the previous chapter, the CE Marking represents the ability of a medical device to meet its essential requirements. The notified bodies review the manufacturer's device applications and the associated technical documentation (Technical Files or Design Dossiers) and allow device manufacturers to affix a CE Marking containing their registration number, once certification is issued. However, what happens when a device manufacturer wrongly affixes a CE Marking to their products? In Monopoly™ land, the penalty would be; "Go directly to jail, do not pass go, do not collect $200.00. Translated into MDD speak, can you say market withdraw? Why should a device manufacturer be concerned with market withdraw for a silly little mistake like accidently placing a CE Mark on unapproved product? Because doing so violates Article 18; and in the EU, violation of the MDD is a violation of EU law. Simply stated; "Their continent, their economic community, their law." Conversely, failing to properly affix a CE Marking onto an approved device package, prior to placing the device into commerce within the EU is also a violation of the Directive. Regardless, failing to comply with Article 18 of the Directive will have a deleterious (look-it-up) effect on the offending device manufacturer; and with that said, Dr. D can confidently state; "Device manufacturers can take that to the proverbial bank."

The MDD – 93/42/EEC

Article 18 – Wrongly CE Marking

Without prejudice to Article 8:

(a) where a Member State establishes that the CE marking has been affixed unduly or is missing in violation of the Directive, the manufacturer or his authorized representative shall be obliged to end the infringement under conditions imposed by the Member State;

(b) where non-compliance continues, the Member State must take all appropriate measures to restrict or prohibit the placing on the market of the product in question or to ensure that it is withdrawn from the market, in accordance with the procedure in Article 8. Those provisions shall also apply where the CE marking has been affixed in accordance with the procedures in this Directive, but inappropriately, on products that are not covered by this Directive.

What You Need to Know

I believe it is time for a Dr. D soapbox moment, "Device manufacturers should never attempt to affix a CE mark to their products until formal approval and certification is received from their notified body!" In fact, product can and will be held at the point of entry into the EU if product has been identified as having a wrongly CE affixed CE Marking. If unapproved product has already entered into the EU, it will need to be withdrawn immediately. Additionally, device manufacturers need to ensure approved product has a CE Mark affixed prior to shipment into the EU. It really becomes a "damned if you do or damned if you don't scenario." Regardless, each Member State retains the authority, under the Directive, to force a market withdraw of product failing to comply with Article 18. Furthermore, the Directive explicitly requires Member States to force the Market Withdraw when violations of Article 18 occur. Finally, a salient point to remember is that once requested to do so by a Member State, market withdraw is the only option for a device manufacturer. There will be no need for further discussion; however, an offending device manufacturer can look forward to hearing from the Competent Authority, from the Member State forcing the market withdraw, and their notified body. The doctor guarantees, these discussions will not be pleasant.

What You Need to Do

Device manufacturers can keep themselves out of trouble by adhering to a couple of basic concepts. Dr. D broken-record time, number one – a device manufacturer should never affix a CE Mark to their product until formal approval and the actual certification is received from their notified body. Number two – device manufacturers should employ effective line-clearance procedures in the packaging and labeling area to ensure that the CE Mark is affixed only to product that has been approved. A strong MRP/ERP System such as SAP™ can facilitate the process, along with well-written work instructions. If an error is made in regards to wrongly affixing or failure to affix a CE Mark is noticed, device manufacturers need to ensure corrective action is pursued immediately. If the device manufacturer notices the error prior to product entry into the EU, they may be able to recover the product and correct the discrepancy; while bypassing the joys of announcing and managing a product recall (what a nasty 6-letter word).

Takeaways

For this chapter, the Doctor will leave the reader with just one takeaway. Broken-record time, again - never affix a CE Mark on device packaging until written approval and certification is received from the device manufacturer's notified body. Let Dr. D repeat, "Never, never, never, ever, affix a CE Mark on device packaging until approval is received!" Why? Because it angers the regulatory gods in the EU, i.e., the Competent Authorities and the notified bodies. As the Incredible Hulk used to say, "You won't like me when I am angry." This saying applies equally to the Competent Authorities.

"A violation of the MDD is a violation of EU law!"

Chapter 23 – *Article 19*

"Decision in Respect of Refusal or Restriction"

Chapter Twenty-three – Article 19

Article 19 of Council Directive 93/42/EEC, a.k.a., the Medical Device Directive (MDD) delineates the requirements for *"Decision in Respect of Refusal or Restriction."* There are few things more frustrating for a device manufacturer then executing a market-withdraw of product. The level of frustration is quickly elevated when they are asked to remove product from the market without being given a definitive reason as to why the market withdraw needs to occur. Equally as frustrating is when a manufacturer's devices are blocked from entering market or additional restrictions enacted. The good news for device manufacturers is that under Article 19 of the Directive, Member States must quickly provide rationale as to why a product withdraw has been mandated, product entry refused, or other restrictions mandated. Additionally, the manufacturer and/or their European Authorized Representative retain the legal right to question the actions through consultation. The bad news is a Member State can mandate an expedited product withdraw due to product safety and efficacy concerns, or the topic of previous chapter, the product in question has a wrongly affixed CE Marking. Either way, the device manufacturer is quickly out of the market in the European Union (EU), resulting in the interruption of the proverbial revenue stream. As Dr. D often states, "Interruption of the revenue stream is a bad thing." Device manufacturers may sometimes view the Competent Authorities in the same light as a truculent (look-it-up) dictator; however, their role is to protect the public health in the respective Member States. It is not a job to be taken lightly.

The MDD – 93/42/EEC

Article 19 – Decision in Respect of Refusal or Restriction

1. Any decision taken pursuant to this Directive:

> *(a) to refuse or restrict the placing on the market or the putting into service of a device or the carrying out of clinical investigations; or*
>
> *(b) to withdraw devices from the market, shall state the exact grounds on which it is based. Such decisions shall be notified without delay to the party concerned, who shall at the same time be informed of the remedies available to him under the national law in force in the Member State in question and of the time limits to which such remedies are subject.*

2. In the event of a decision as referred to in paragraph 1, the manufacturer, or his authorized representative, shall have an opportunity to put forward his viewpoint in advance, unless such consultation is not possible because of the urgency of the measure to be taken.

What You Need to Know

There are two salient concepts device manufacturers need to grasp. The first concept is a Member State needs to provide the actual grounds driving the decisions made in regards to market withdraws, refusals, or restrictions. The second concept is that device manufacturers have some recourse in regards to addressing decisions made by a Member State; and that process is vetted through consultation. Hopefully, the manufacturer is consulted in advance of a Member State's decision. However, device manufacturers should understand that if a Member State decides that there is a significant urgency needed for a market-withdraw of product, an advance consultation with the device manufacturer and/or their authorized rep, may not always be possible. Can you say, "Interruption of revenue stream?" Regardless, Article 19 does provide an avenue for two-communications between Member States and device manufacturers when issues result in potential market withdraws, refusals, or restrictions in the EU.

What You Need to Do

Dr. D is going to let the readers in on a not-so-well-kept secret. The secret is, "device manufacturers need to design and manufacture devices that are "safe, effective, and compliant" with their essential requirements, while being properly certified by their notified body!" An easy way to remember the three-key elements of the doctor's secret is the acronym "SEC." Yes, Dr. D knows this acronym is already used by the Securities and Exchange Commission and the Southeastern Conference. That being said, SEC also stands for "Safe, Effective, and Compliant." The doctor likes his acronym better. The entire process commences with a robust design that is properly validated. The process continues with the execution of clinical trials (if appropriate) to determine if the finished medical device is safe and effective. The entire process culminates with review and approval of the technical file or design dossier by the notified body and the formal issuance of certification. If shortcuts are taken, receiving approval from your notified body will be problematic. Dr. D guarantees it!

Takeaways

For this chapter, the doctor will leave the readers with two takeaways. Dr. D also would like to apologize in advance for his broken-record approach to drive home salient points; however, this approach worked when the doctor was a United States Marine (repetitive bouts of pain), and continues to be an effective approach today. That said, (1) in accordance with Article 19, Member States must provide rationale in regards to decisions made that result in market withdraws, refusals, and restrictions. (2) Device manufacturers and/or their authorized rep shall have the opportunity to consult with the

Member State in regards to the decisions made.

"Interruption of the revenue stream is a bad thing"

Chapter 24 – *Article 20*

"Confidentiality"

Chapter Twenty-four – Article 20

Article 20 of Council Directive 93/42/EEC, a.k.a., the Medical Device Directive (MDD) delineates the requirements for *"Confidentiality."* Confidentially speaking, Article 20 of the Directive is all about disclosure, or should Dr. D say, limited disclosure. So what does that mean Dr. D? Basically, Article 19 of the Directive requires that all parties involved with executing their duties in accordance with the Directive, treat all information obtained as confidential, where applicable. However, Member States, their Competent Authorities, and the notified bodies have the right to disseminate information such as: (a) warnings; (b) registration of persons or organizations involved in the placement of devices into the EU (ref. Article 14); (c) information sent to a device manufacturer, their authorized representative, and their distributor when incidents occur (ref. Article 10); and (d) data relating to certificates. That being said, the only significant piece of confidentiality remaining is the Intellectual Property (IP). Considering a device manufacturer is required to provide significant granularity in regards to design, development, validation testing, verification testing, and clinical trials (if applicable) to their notified body through the submission of Technical Files and Design Dossiers; there really is not much left on the proverbial table in regards to confidentiality and the dissemination of information (the doctor's opinion). Regardless of the opinion of Dr. D and his concerns surrounding the all-inclusive handling of confidentiality of a device manufacturer's data, the same opinion and concerns could be formed, mutatis mutandis (look-it-up), by the notified bodies. Remember, the notified bodies work for the device manufacturers but they must answer to the Competent Authorities, from whom they receive their power.

The MDD – 93/42/EEC

Article 20 – Confidentiality

1. Without prejudice to the existing national provisions and practices on medical confidentiality, Member States shall ensure that all the Parties involved in the application of this Directive are bound to observe confidentiality with regard to all information obtained in carrying out their tasks. This does not affect the obligation of Member States and notified bodies with regard to mutual information and the dissemination of warnings, nor the obligations of the persons concerned to provide information under criminal law.

2. The following information shall not be treated as confidential:
(a) information on the registration of persons responsible for placing devices on the market in accordance with Article 14;
(b) information to users sent out by the manufacturer, authorized representative or distributor in relation to a measure according to Article 10(3);
(c) information contained in certificates issued, modified, supplemented, suspended or withdrawn.

3. The measures designed to amend non-essential elements of this Directive, inter alia by supplementing it, relating to determination of the conditions under which other information may be made publicly available, and in particular for Class IIb and Class III devices to any obligation for manufacturers to prepare and make available a summary of the information and data related to the device, shall be adopted in accordance with the regulatory procedure with scrutiny referred to in Article7 (3).

What You Need to Know

Device manufacturers need to know that proprietary information, for the most part, is protected under the Directive. However, if a device's safety and efficacy become a concern within the EU, or a specific Member State finds the dissemination of a warning necessary, the Member State, Competent Authority, and notified body shall retain the right to exchange mutual information. Remember, under the Directive regulatory bodies operating within the EU are obligated to take the appropriate action in order to protect public health. Additionally, the Directive is very specific in regard to the type of information that **is not protected** under the confidentiality clause. The three salient categories of information not protected under the Directive are; (a) registration information, (b) user information, and (c) certification information. Furthermore, there is what the doctor considers a "catch-all" element under the confidentiality clause. Section 3 of the clause expands on the other information being made available publically. For example, it is not out of the question or the realm of the Directive for manufacturers to provide a summary of information and relevant data associated with a device entered into commerce within the EU. This holds particularly true for the higher-risk category devices such as a Class IIb or a Class III. Finally, when in doubt device manufacturers should always confide in the notified bodies. Why? Dr. D broken-record time, "Because the notified bodies work for the device manufacturers." Although, Dr. D has on occasion been witness to the obverse, when notified bodies believe they are the client. When that happens, all that is usually required is a simple reminder as to who is actually signing the proverbial checks.

What You Need to Do

Dr. D always recommends that an organization develop a written policy for handling of all information, data, records, etc. A non-disclosure agreement (NDA) should always be part of the policy. The doctor would also like to remind the reader that a contract/written agreement should also be in place for the device manufacturer's European Authorized Representative. When device issues occur in the EU, and trust Dr. D when I say they will occur, the authorized rep will be the device manufacturer's first line of defense. It is imperative that the manufacturer, the authorized rep, and the notified body be on the exact same page in regards to the dissemination of information and disclosure. Another salient point that device manufacturers need to grasp is that the Competent Authorities are regulatory gods within the EU. If a device is hurting people and an abundance of vigilance reports places the safety and efficacy of a device into question, the Competent Authorities have the legal right to any and all information associated with the device, including the technical file or design dossier, and all of the supporting reports. How does the doctor know this? Because Dr. D has lived through the pain of having to review an entire dossier with the Competent Authority of a Member State. It was an extremely painful experience, but it was also a fabulous learning experience. One final note, the technical content of the technical file or design dossier is never to be shared with the general public. Regardless of the Directive, that is why the NDA is an important document.

Takeaways

For this chapter, the doctor will leave the readers with three final thoughts.

1. Under the Directive, reasonable attempts at confidentiality are required to be sustained.

2. There are three categories of information that are not protected under the confidentiality clause; registration, user, and certification information.

3. The best way an organization can protect itself in regards to the managing of proprietary information is through a well-documented policy augmented by the NDA.

"Proprietary information, for the most part, is protected under the Directive"

Chapter 25 – *Article 20a*

"Cooperation"

Chapter Twenty-five – Article 20a

Article 20a of Council Directive 93/42/EEC, a.k.a., the Medical Device Directive (MDD)

delineates the requirements for *"Cooperation."* Using the term cooperation in regards to

a standard, law, regulation, or in the case of the MDD, a Directive, almost sounds like an

oxymoron not unlike "military intelligence" or one of my favorites "genuine-artificial

jumbo-shrimp." What? Cooperation? Stealing a line from Dick Vitale, "Are you kidding

me!" All kidding aside, Dr. D loves the concept, although attempting to get all of the

Competent Authorities, from 27-Member States to cooperate, is clearly a daunting task.

In fact, achieving cooperation with a small, diverse, and opinionated group does not often

lend itself to being an efficacious (look-it-up) approach for exchanging information and

proactively developing solutions. The doctor emphatically believes there will always be

disagreements and misunderstanding in pursuit of cooperation. It really boils down to the

fundamentals of basic group dynamics.

The MDD – 93/42/EEC

Article 20a – Cooperation

Member States shall take appropriate measures to ensure that the competent authorities of the Member States cooperate with each other and with the Commission and transmit to each other the information necessary to enable this Directive to be applied uniformly. The Commission shall provide for the organization of an exchange of experience between the competent authorities responsible for market surveillance in order to coordinate the uniform application of this Directive. Without prejudice to the provisions of this Directive, cooperation may be part of initiatives developed at an international level

What You Need to Know

Under the Directive, Competent Authorities are required to cooperate when

disseminating information relevant to the Directive. In fact, the Commission provides a forum for the organization and exchange of information between the Competent Authorities. The need for Member States to cooperate is an important cornerstone when it comes to post-market surveillance activities for the European Union (EU). In fact, trust Dr. D when I say, "The sharing of post-market surveillance data by the Competent Authorities has exhibited a dramatic improvement in recent years." A good example of this cooperation can be seen in a recently developed tool, the EU's database for capturing Vigilance Reporting Data (Medical Devices Sector – Implementation Vigilance Competent Authorities Notification Reports). Remember, the foundation for the post-market surveillance system in Europe is the Vigilance Report; and cooperation between the Competent Authorities facilitates the dissemination of post-market surveillance data.

What You Need to Do

As a device manufacturer, you need to understand the requirement that the Competent Authorities are obligated to cooperate in accordance with the Directive. A pragmatic approach for the sharing of information ensures that medical devices that are not safe and effective are quickly identified and removed from the European market. Can you say Recall (Dr. D's favorite-nasty little 6-letter word). If a device manufacturer is marketing devices that are safe and effective, while complying with all aspects of the Directive, there will never be a reason to worry in regards to Article 20a. It will be nothing more than just another clause. One salient point to remember is that the cooperation between the Competent Authorities is not limited to post-market surveillance. Article 20a requires that cooperation be extended toward all aspects of the MDD, in support of a uniform application of the Directive. The "all-encompassing support concept" makes Article 20a an extremely powerful clause indeed.

Takeaways

For this chapter, the doctor will leave the readers with just one takeaway. The Directive requires the Competent Authorities, from each of the Member States, to cooperate – period! Remember, the Competent Authorities are becoming very proficient in the art of cooperation.

"The sharing of Vigilance Report information by the Competent Authorities has improved greatly."

Chapter 26 – *Article 21*

"Repeal and Amendment of

Directives"

Chapter Twenty-six – Article 21

Article 21 of Council Directive 93/42/EEC, a.k.a., the Medical Device Directive (MDD) delineates the requirements for *"Repeal and Amendment of Directives."* Under Article 21, medical device manufacturers retain the right to repeal or amend any of the Directives they just do not like or wish to comply. Dr. D is just kidding; however, I do believe the doctor has your undivided attention. Simply put, Article 21 delineates the repeal and actual changes made to Directives and Articles within the Directives, period. That being said, the guidance provided for this chapter will be extremely brief. There really is no need for interpretation or an in-depth understanding of Article 21, other than it exists and provides granularity in regards to changes made to Directives. Not wanting the readers to take the axiomatic (look-it-up) principles of the MDD for granted, Dr. D always recommends reading the Articles of the Directive, regardless of their perceived applicability to a device manufacturer's quality management system (QMS).

The MDD – 93/42/EEC

Article 21 – Repeal and Amendment of Directives

1. Directive 76/764/EEC is hereby repealed with effect from 1 January 1995.

2. In the title and Article 1 of Directive 84/539/EEC, 'human or' is deleted. In Article 2 of Directive 84/539/EEC, the following subparagraph is added to paragraph 1: 'If the appliance is at the same time a medical device within the meaning of Directive 93/42/EEC (*) and if it satisfies the essential requirements laid down therein for that device, the device shall be deemed to be in conformity with the requirements of this Directive.

3. Directive 90/385/EEC is hereby amended as follows:

> *1. In Article 1 (2) the following two subparagraphs are added:'*
> *(h) "placing on the market" means the first making available in return for payment or free of charge of a device other than a device intended for clinical investigation, with a view to distribution and/or use on the Community market, regardless of whether it is new or fully refurbished;*
>
> *(i) "manufacturer" means the natural or legal person with responsibility for the*

design, manufacture, packaging and labeling of a device before it is placed on the market under his own name, regardless of whether these operations are carried out by that person himself or on his behalf by a third party. The obligations of this Directive to be met by manufacturers also apply to the natural or legal person who assembles, packages, processes, fully refurbishes and/or labels one or more ready-made products and/or assigns to them their intended purpose as a device with a view to their being placed on the market under his own name. This subparagraph does not apply to the person who, while not a manufacturer within the meaning of the first subparagraph, assembles or adapts devices already on the market to their intended purpose for an individual patient;

2. In Article 9 the following paragraphs are added:

5. During the conformity assessment procedure for a device, the manufacturer and/or the notified body shall take account of the results of any assessment and verification operations which, where appropriate, have been carried out in accordance with this Directive at an intermediate stage of manufacture.

6. Where the conformity assessment procedure involves the intervention of a notified body, the manufacturer, or his authorized representative established in the Community, may apply to a body of his choice within the framework of the tasks for which the body has been notified.

7. The notified body may require, where duly justified, any information or data which is necessary for establishing and maintaining the attestation of conformity in view of the chosen procedure.

8. Decisions taken by the notified bodies in accordance with Annexes II and III shall be valid for a maximum of five years and maybe extended on application, made at a time agreed in the contract signed by both parties, for further periods of five years.

9. By derogation from paragraphs 1 and 2 the competent authorities may authorize, on duly justified request, the placing on the market and putting into service, within the territory of the Member State concerned, of individual devices for which the procedures referred to in paragraphs 1 and 2 have not been carried out and the use of which is in the interest of protection of health.'

3. The following Article 9a is inserted after Article 9: 'Article 9a

1. Where a Member State considers that the conformity of a device or family of devices should be established, by way of derogation from the provisions of Article 9, by applying solely one of the given procedures chosen from among those referred to in Article 9, it shall submit a duly substantiated request to the Commission and ask it to take the necessary measures. These measures shall be adopted in accordance with the procedure referred to in Article 7 (2) of Directive 93/42/EEC (*).

2. The Commission shall inform the Member States of the measures taken and, where appropriate, publish the relevant parts of these measures in the Official Journal of the European Communities.

4. Article 10 shall be amended as follows: —the following subparagraph shall be added to paragraph 2: 'Member States may however authorize manufacturers to start the clinical investigations in question before the expiry of the 60- day period, provided that the Ethical Committee concerned has delivered a favorable opinion with respect to the investigation program in question. ', —the following paragraph shall be inserted: '2a. The authorization referred to in the second subparagraph of paragraph 2 maybe subject to approval by the competent authority';

5. The following is added to Article 14: 'In the event of a decision as referred to in the previous paragraph the manufacturer, or his authorized representative established in the Community, shall have an opportunity to put forward his viewpoint in advance, unless such consultation is not possible because of the urgency of the measures to be taken. '

What You Need to Know

Hopefully, all device manufacturers have taken the appropriate steps to ensure all of the amendments to the MDD, which went into force in March of 2010, have been incorporated into their businesses. If not, I am sure the notified bodies, for the offending device manufacturers, have reacted accordingly through the issuance of major deviations. Regardless, device manufacturers need to know and understand that Article 21 delineates the changes made to Directives. Yes – I know Dr. D once again sounds like that proverbial broken record; however, the doctor's message is clear; "Compliance to all Articles of the MDD is not optional. Compliance is mandated by law"

What You Need to Do

Broken-record-time again, "Device manufacturers need to read and understand all of Articles associated with the MDD." As the doctor alluded to in the previous paragraph, if a device manufacturer has been proactive and worked toward compliance with the revised MDD and all of the Articles, then there will not be any issues. For device manufacturers that still find themselves on the "south-side" of compliance, what in the heck are you waiting for, compliance pixie dust? Dr. D strongly suggests that device manufacturers perform a quick sanity check in regards ensuring all of the changes depicted in Article 21 have been adequately addressed within your organizations.

Takeaways

Similar to the last chapter, the doctor will leave the readers with just one takeaway. Article 21 of the MDD delineates the repeal of and amendments to Directives. It is incumbent upon device manufacturers to ensure all of these changes have been captured and adequately addressed within their organizations. If your organization has not implemented these changes; Dr. D suggests you "Get er done," thank you Larry the Cable Guy for those famous words of wisdom.

"Compliance to the MDD is Mandatory under the Laws of the EU!"

Chapter 27 – *Articles 22 & 23*

"Implementation, Transitional Provisions"

Chapter Twenty-seven – Articles 22 & 23

In this chapter, the doctor will provide guidance for the final two Articles associated with Council Directive 93/42/EEC, a.k.a., the Medical Device Directive (MDD). Article 22 of the MDD delineates the requirements for *"Implementation, Transitional Provisions."* Simply put, Article 22 mandates that Member States are required to comply with the MDD no later than 01 July 1994. Now Dr. D believes it is a pretty safe bet to assume that 17-years, after the fact, Member States are complying with this Directive. Article 23 of the MDD, contains no formal title. That being said, Dr. D refers to this Article as the "Formal Address Clause." As for Article 23, it contains one eight-word sentence; *"This Directive is addressed to the Member States."* Because Article 23 is so eloquently simple, the doctor will provide just one piece of guidance for this Article. It is not addressed to device manufacturers, it is addressed to Member States; and no the doctor is not trying to be a wise guy (well maybe just a little). All kidding aside, just because Article 23 is addressed to Member States; it does not mean device manufacturers do not have to comply with the Directive. Remember, the MDD is not a piece of supposititious (look-it-up) legislation but the law within the European Union (EU) and compliance is mandatory.

The MDD – 93/42/EEC

Article 22 – Implementation, Transitional Provisions

1. Member States shall adopt and publish the laws, regulations and administrative provisions necessary to comply with this Directive not later than 1 July 1994. They shall immediately inform the Commission thereof. The Standing Committee referred to in Article 7 may assume its tasks from the date of notification (1) of this Directive. The Member States may take the measures referred to in Article 16 on notification of this Directive. When Member States adopt these provisions, these shall contain a reference to this Directive or shall be accompanied by such a reference at the time of their official publication. The procedure for such reference shall be adopted by Member States. Member States shall apply these provisions with effect from 1 January 1995.

2. Member States shall communicate to the Commission the texts of the provisions of national law which they adopt in the field covered by this Directive.

3. Member States shall take the necessary action to ensure that the notified bodies which are responsible pursuant to Article 11 (1) to (5) for conformity assessment take account of any relevant information regarding the characteristics and performance of such devices, including in particular the results of any relevant tests and verification already carried out under preexisting national law, regulations or administrative provisions in respect of such devices.

4. Member States shall accept: —devices which conform to the rules in force in their territory on 31 December 1994 being placed on the market during a period of five years following the adoption of this Directive, and —the aforementioned devices being put into service until 30 June 2001 at the latest. In the case of devices which have been subjected to EEC pattern approval in accordance with Directive 76/764/EEC, Member States shall accept their being placed on the market and put into service during the period up to 30 June 2004.

Article 23 – "Note: There is no title"

This Directive is addressed to the Member States.

What You Need to Know

Article 22 is broken down into four components that are directed at the Member States. The first component prescribes the need for Member States to *"adopt and publish the laws, regulations, and administrative provisions"* before the drop-dead date of 01 July 1994. Simply stated, compliance to the Directive is mandatory by the July date. The second component of Article 22 is a requirement for Member States to communicate the provisions made in regard to national law, in support of this Directive, back to the Commission. The third and fourth components of Article 22, at the time of the initial release of the Directive, did have the potential to influence medical device manufacturers and the devices they entered into commerce within the EU. Specifically, the third component of Article 22 directed Member States to ensure notified bodies reevaluated devices approved under national standards and the relevancy of testing and verification activities previously performed. The fourth and final component of Article 22 directed Member States to grant approval for devices that conformed to their country-specific rules in place on 31 December 1994. The Directive delineated a five-year period, *"following the adoption of this Directive."* So Dr. D what does all of this really mean? In short, Article 22 really has no impact on device manufacturers today. The dates critical to device manufacturers have long passed; and the first two components of Article 22 are directed at the Member States.

As depicted in the introduction for this chapter, Article 23 is addressed to Member States. Device manufacturers need to know that there are 23 Articles associated with the Directive; however, Article 23 does not impact device manufacturers. In fact, since Article 23 is so simple, you may want to impress your friends by being able to recite an entire Article from memory. Then again, what would be the point?

What You Need to Do

I love it when the good doctor has the opportunity to say; "Device Manufacturers have nothing to do or worry about in regards to these Articles." Once again folks, Dr. D will climb to the top of his soapbox and commence with the broken-record speak. Compliance to the Directive is mandatory; however, not all of the Articles apply directly to Device Manufacturers. That being said, all of the provisions depicted in Article 22 that may have influenced a device manufacturer's product being in the EU have long-since expired. The other requirements mandated by Article 22 are Member State centric. As for the very complex and succinct Article 23, it is directed to Member States, period.

Takeaways

For this chapter, the doctor will leave just one piece of guidance, "forgetta-bout-it" (a quote made famous by James Gandolfini – a.k.a., Tony Soprano). Seriously, device manufacturers need to know that there are 23 Articles; however, in regards to Articles 22 and 23, they have zero influence on device manufacturers so please, just "forgetta-bout-it."

"Compliance to the Directive is mandatory; however, not all of the Articles apply directly to Device Manufacturers."

Chapter 28 – *Annex I*
"Essential Requirements"

Chapter Twenty-eight – Annex I

Since the beginning of this book, Dr. D has been reviewing and providing guidance for the 23-Articles that for the foundation for Council Directive 93/42/EEC, a.k.a., the Medical Device Directive (MDD). Understanding these Articles and the imbedded regulations is extremely important for device manufacturers; however, it is the opinion of the good doctor, the Annexes associated with the MDD is where the proverbial rubber hits the road. Device manufacturers already shipping into the European Union (EU) understand the ramifications of having products that fail to meet essential requirements or a quality management system (QMS) failing to meet the requirements detailed within these annexes. All one has to do is glance quickly over the certifications, issued by their notified bodies, to understand the significance of these Annexes. Since Dr. D never likes to be vituperated (look-it-up), and I am sure the readers would not enjoy being vituperated by their boss or peers; the doctor will spend the next 12-chapters enlightening readers on the salient points associated with Annexes I through XII. In this chapter, Dr. D will commence with the review and guidance for complying with Annex I of the MDD, "Essential Requirements."

The MDD – 93/42/EEC

ANNEX I – Essential Requirements

I. GENERAL REQUIREMENTS

> *1. The devices must be designed and manufactured in such a way that, when used under the conditions and for the purposes intended, they will not compromise the clinical condition or the safety of patients, or the safety and health of users or, where applicable, other persons, provided that any risks which may be associated with their intended use constitute acceptable risks when weighed against the benefits to the patient and are compatible with a high level of protection of health and safety.*

> *This shall include:*

- *reducing, as far as possible, the risk of use error due to the ergonomic features of the device and the environment in which the device is intended to be used (design for patient safety), and*

- *consideration of the technical knowledge, experience, education and training and where applicable the medical and physical conditions of intended users (design for lay, professional, disabled or other users).*

2. The solutions adopted by the manufacturer for the design and construction of the devices must conform to safety principles, taking account of the generally acknowledged state of the art.

In selecting the most appropriate solutions, the manufacturer must apply the following principles in the following order:
- eliminate or reduce risks as far as possible (inherently safe design and construction),

- where appropriate take adequate protection measures including alarms if necessary, in relation to risks that cannot be eliminated,

- inform users of the residual risks due to any shortcomings of the protection measures adopted.

3. The devices must achieve the performances intended by the manufacturer and be designed, manufactured and packaged in such a way that they are suitable for one or more of the functions referred to in Article1 (2) (a), as specified by the manufacturer.

4. The characteristics and performances referred to in Sections 1, 2 and 3 must not be adversely affected to such a degree that the clinical conditions and safety of the patients and, where applicable, of other persons are compromised during the lifetime of the device as indicated by the manufacturer, when the device is subjected to the stresses which can occur during normal conditions of use.

5. The devices must be designed, manufactured and packed in such a way that their characteristics and performances during their intended use will not be adversely affected during transport and storage taking account of the instructions and information provided by the manufacturer.

6. Any undesirable side-effect must constitute an acceptable risk when weighed against the performances intended.

6a. Demonstration of conformity with the essential requirements must include a clinical evaluation in accordance with Annex X.

II. REQUIREMENTS REGARDING DESIGN AND CONSTRUCTION

7. Chemical, physical and biological properties

7.1. The devices must be designed and manufactured in such a way as to guarantee the characteristics and performances referred to in Section I on the 'General requirements'. Particular attention must be paid to:

- the choice of materials used, particularly as regards toxicity and, where appropriate, flammability,

- the compatibility between the materials used and biological tissues, cells and body fluids, taking account of the intended purpose of the device,

- where appropriate, the results of biophysical or modeling research whose validity has been demonstrated beforehand.

7.2. The devices must be designed, manufactured and packed in such a way as to minimize the risk posed by contaminants and residues to the persons involved in the transport, storage and use of the devices and to the patients, taking account of the intended purpose of the product. Particular attention must be paid to the tissues exposed and to the duration and frequency of exposure.

7.3. The devices must be designed and manufactured in such a way that they can be used safely with the materials, substances and gases with which they enter into contact during their normal use or during routine procedures; if the devices are intended to administer medicinal products they must be designed and manufactured in such a way as to be compatible with the medicinal products concerned according to the provisions and restrictions governing these products and that their performance is maintained in accordance with the intended use.

7.4. Where a device incorporates, as an integral part, a substance which, if used separately, maybe considered to be a medicinal product as defined in Article 1 of Directive 2001/83/EC and which is liable to act upon the body with action ancillary to that of the device, the quality, safety and usefulness of the substance must be verified by analogy with the methods specified in Annex I to Directive 2001/83/ EC.

For the substances referred to in the first paragraph, the notified body shall, having verified the usefulness of the substance as part of the medical device and taking account of the intended purpose of the device, seek a scientific opinion from one of the competent authorities designated by the Member States or the European Medicines Agency (EMEA) acting particularly through its committee in accordance with Regulation (EC) No 726/2004 (1) on the quality and safety of the substance including the clinical benefit/risk profile of the incorporation of the substance into the device. When issuing its opinion, the competent authority or the EMEA shall take into account the manufacturing process and the data related to the usefulness of incorporation of the substance into the device as determined by the notified body.

Where a device incorporates, as an integral part, a human blood derivative, the notified body shall, having verified the usefulness of the substance as part of the medical device and taking into account the intended purpose of the device, seek a scientific opinion from the EMEA, acting particularly through its committee, on the quality and safety of the substance including the clinical benefit/risk profile of the incorporation of the human blood derivative into the device. When issuing its opinion, the EMEA shall take into account the manufacturing process and the data related to the usefulness of incorporation of the substance into the device as determined by the notified body.

Where changes are made to an ancillary substance incorporated in a device, in particular related to its manufacturing process, the notified body shall be informed of the changes and shall consult the relevant medicines competent authority (i.e. the one involved in the initial consultation), in order to confirm that the quality and safety of the ancillary substance are maintained. The competent authority shall take into account the data related to the usefulness of incorporation of the substance into the device as determined by the notified body, in order to ensure that the changes have no negative impact on the established benefit/risk profile of the addition of the substance in the medical device.

When the relevant medicines competent authority (i.e. the one involved in the initial consultation) has obtained information on the ancillary substance, which could have an impact on the established benefit/risk profile of the addition of the substance in the medical device, it shall provide the notified body with advice, whether this information has an impact on the established benefit/risk profile of the addition of the substance in the medical device or not. The notified body shall take the updated scientific opinion into account in reconsidering its assessment of the conformity assessment procedure.

7.5. The devices must be designed and manufactured in such a way as to reduce to a minimum the risks posed by substances leaking from the device. Special attention shall be given to substances which are carcinogenic, mutagenic or toxic to reproduction, in accordance with Annex I to Council Directive 67/548/EEC of 27 June 1967 on the approximation of laws, regulations and administrative provisions relating to the classification, packaging and labeling of dangerous substances (1).

If parts of a device (or a device itself) intended to administer and/or remove medicines, body liquids or other substances to or from the body, or devices intended for transport and storage of such body fluids or substances, contain phthalates which are classified as carcinogenic, mutagenic or toxic to reproduction, of category 1 or 2, in accordance with Annex I to Directive 67/548/EEC, these devices must be labeled on the device itself and/or on the packaging for each unit or, where appropriate, on the sales packaging as a device containing phthalates.

If the intended use of such devices includes treatment of children or treatment of pregnant or nursing women, the manufacturer must provide a specific justification for the use of these substances with regard to compliance with the essential requirements, in particular of this paragraph, within the technical documentation and, within the instructions for use, information on residual risks for these patient groups and, if applicable, on appropriate precautionary measures.

7.6. Devices must be designed and manufactured in such a way as to reduce, as much as possible, risks posed by the unintentional ingress of substances into the device taking into account the device and the nature of the environment in which it is intended to be used.

8. *Infection and microbial contamination*

8.1. The devices and manufacturing processes must be designed in such a way as to eliminate or reduce as far as possible the risk of infection to the patient, user and third parties. The design must allow easy handling and, where necessary, minimize contamination of the device by the patient or vice versa during use.

8.2. Tissues of animal origin must originate from animals that have been subjected to veterinary controls and surveillance adapted to the intended use of the tissues.

Notified bodies shall retain information on the geographical origin of the animals.

Processing, preservation, testing and handling of tissues, cells and substances of animal origin must be carried out so as to provide optimal security. In particular safety with regard to viruses and other transmissible agents must be addressed by implementation of validated methods of elimination or viral inactivation in the course of the manufacturing process.

8.3. Devices delivered in a sterile state must be designed, manufactured and packed in a non-reusable pack and/or according to appropriate procedures to ensure that they are sterile when placed on the market and remain sterile, under the storage and transport conditions laid down, until the protective packaging is damaged or opened.

8.4. Devices delivered in a sterile state must have been manufactured and sterilized by an appropriate, validated method.

8.5. Devices intended to be sterilized must be manufactured inappropriately controlled (e. g. environmental) conditions.

8.6. Packaging systems for non-sterile devices must keep the product without deterioration at the level of cleanliness stipulated and, if the devices are to be sterilized prior to use, minimize the risk of microbial contamination; the packaging system must be suitable taking account of the method of sterilization indicated by the manufacturer.

8.7. The packaging and/or label of the device must distinguish between identical or similar products sold in both sterile and non-sterile condition.

9. *Construction and environmental properties*

9.1. If the device is intended for use in combination with other devices or equipment, the whole combination, including the connection system must be safe and must not impair the specified performances of the devices. Any restrictions on use must be indicated on the label or in the instructions for use.

9.2. Devices must be designed and manufactured in such a way as to remove or minimize as far as is possible:
—the risk of injury, in connection with their physical features, including the volume/pressure ratio, dimensional and where appropriate ergonomic features,

—risks connected with reasonably foreseeable environmental conditions, such as magnetic fields, external electrical influences, electrostatic discharge,

pressure, temperature or variations in pressure and acceleration,

—the risks of reciprocal interference with other devices normally used in the investigations or for the treatment given,

—risks arising where maintenance or calibration are not possible (as with implants), from ageing of materials used or loss of accuracy of any measuring or control mechanism.

9.3. Devices must be designed and manufactured in such a way as to minimize the risks of fire or explosion during normal use and in single fault condition. Particular attention must be paid to devices whose intended use includes exposure to flammable substances or to substances which could cause combustion.

10. Devices with a measuring function

10.1. Devices with a measuring function must be designed and manufactured in such a way as to provide sufficient accuracy and stability within appropriate limits of accuracy and taking account of the intended purpose of the device. The limits of accuracy must be indicated by the manufacturer.

10.2. The measurement, monitoring and display scale must be designed in line with ergonomic principles, taking account of the intended purpose of the device.

10.3. The measurements made by devices with a measuring function must be expressed in legal units conforming to the provisions of Council Directive 80/181/EEC (1).

11. Protection against radiation

11.1. General

> *11.1.1. Devices shall be designed and manufactured in such a way that exposure of patients, users and other persons to radiation shall be reduced as far as possible compatible with the intended purpose, whilst not restricting the application of appropriate specified levels for therapeutic and diagnostic purposes.*

11.2. Intended radiation

> *11.2.1. Where devices are designed to emit hazardous levels of radiation necessary for a specific medical purpose the benefit of which is considered to outweigh the risks inherent in the emission, it must be possible for the user to control the emissions. Such devices shall be designed and manufactured to ensure reproducibility and tolerance of relevant variable parameters.*

> *11.2.2. Where devices are intended to emit potentially hazardous, visible and/ or invisible radiation, they must be fitted, where practicable, with visual displays and/or audible warnings of such emissions.*

11.3. Unintended radiation

11.3.1. Devices shall be designed and manufactured in such a way that exposure of patients, users and other persons to the emission of unintended, stray or scattered radiation is reduced as far as possible.

11.4. Instructions

11.4.1. The operating instructions for devices emitting radiation must give detailed information as to the nature of the emitted radiation, means of protecting the patient and the user and on ways of avoiding misuse and of eliminating the risks inherent in installation.

11.5. Ionizing radiation

11.5.1. Devices intended to emit ionizing radiation must be designed and manufactured in such a way as to ensure that, where practicable, the quantity, geometry and quality of radiation emitted can be varied and controlled taking into account the intended use.

11.5.2. Devices emitting ionizing radiation intended for diagnostic radiology shall be designed and manufactured in such a way as to achieve appropriate image and/or output quality for the intended medical purpose whilst minimizing radiation exposure of the patient and user.

11.5.3. Devices emitting ionizing radiation, intended for therapeutic radiology shall be designed and manufactured in such a way as to enable reliable monitoring and control of the delivered dose, the beam type and energy and where appropriate the quality of radiation.

12. *Requirements for medical devices connected to or equipped with an energy source*

12.1. Devices incorporating electronic programmable systems must be designed to ensure the repeatability, reliability and performance of these systems according to the intended use. In the event of a single fault condition (in the system) appropriate means should be adopted to eliminate or reduce as far as possible consequent risks.

12.1a For devices which incorporate software or which are medical software in themselves, the software must be validated according to the state of the art taking into account the principles of development lifecycle, risk management, validation and verification.

12.2. Devices where the safety of the patients depends on an internal power supply must be equipped with a means of determining the state of the power supply.

12.3. Devices where the safety of the patients depends on an external power supply must include an alarm system to signal any power failure.

12.4. Devices intended to monitor one or more clinical parameters of a patient must be equipped with appropriate alarm systems to alert the user of situations which could lead to death or severe deterioration of the patient's state of health.

12.5. Devices must be designed and manufactured in such a way as to minimize the risks of creating electromagnetic fields which could impair the operation of other devices or equipment in the usual environment.

12.6. Protection against electrical risks Devices must be designed and manufactured in such a way as to avoid, as far as possible, the risk of accidental electric shocks during normal use and in single fault condition, provided the devices are installed correctly.

12.7. Protection against mechanical and thermal risks

12.7.1. Devices must be designed and manufactured in such a way as to protect the patient and user against mechanical risks connected with, for example, resistance, stability and moving parts.

12.7.2. Devices must be designed and manufactured in such a way as to reduce to the lowest possible level the risks arising from vibration generated by the devices, taking account of technical progress and of the means available for limiting vibrations, particularly at source, unless the vibrations are part of the specified performance.

12.7.3. Devices must be designed and manufactured in such a way as to reduce to the lowest possible level the risks arising from the noise emitted, taking account of technical progress and of the means available to reduce noise, particularly at source, unless the noise emitted is part of the specified performance.

12.7.4. Terminals and connectors to the electricity, gas or hydraulic and pneumatic energy supplies which the user has to handle must be designed and constructed in such a way as to minimize all possible risks.

12.7.5. Accessible parts of the devices (excluding the parts or areas intended to supply heat or reach given temperatures) and their surroundings must not attain potentially dangerous temperatures under normal use.

12.8. Protection against the risks posed to the patient by energy supplies or substances

12.8.1. Devices for supplying the patient with energy or substances must be designed and constructed in such a way that the flow-rate can beset and maintained accurately enough to guarantee the safety of the patient and of the user.

12.8.2. Devices must be fitted with the means of preventing and/or indicating any inadequacies in the flow-rate which could pose a danger. Devices must incorporate suitable means to prevent, as far as possible, the accidental release of dangerous levels of energy from an energy and/or substance source.

12.9. The function of the controls and indicators must be clearly specified on the devices. Where a device bears instructions required for its operation or indicates operating or adjustment parameters by means of a visual system, such information must be understandable to the user and, as appropriate, the patient.

13. *Information supplied by the manufacturer*

13.1. Each device must be accompanied by the information needed to use it safely and properly, taking account of the training and knowledge of the potential users, and to identify the manufacturer.

This information comprises the details on the label and the data in the instructions for use.

As far as practicable and appropriate, the information needed to use the device safely must be set out on the device itself and/or on the packaging for each unit or, where appropriate, on the sales packaging. If individual packaging of each unit is not practicable, the information must be set out in the leaflet supplied with one or more devices.

Instructions for use must be included in the packaging for every device. By way of exception, no such instructions for use are needed for devices in Class I or IIa if they can be used safely without any such instructions.

13.2. Where appropriate, this information should take the form of symbols. Any symbol or identification color used must conform to the harmonized standards. In areas for which no standards exist, the symbols and colors must be described in the documentation supplied with the device.

13.3. The label must bear the following particulars:

> *(a) the name or trade name and address of the manufacturer. For devices imported into the Community, in view of their distribution in the Community, the label, or the outer packaging, or instructions for use, shall contain in addition the name and address of the authorized representative where the manufacturer does not have a registered place of business in the Community;*

> *(b) the details strictly necessary to identify the device and the contents of the packaging especially for the users;*

> *(c) where appropriate, the word 'STERILE';*

> *(d) where appropriate, the batch code, preceded by the word 'LOT', or the serial number;*

> *(e) where appropriate, an indication of the date by which the device should be used, in safety, expressed as the year and month;*

> *(f) where appropriate, an indication that the device is for single use. A manufacturer's indication of single use must be consistent across the Community;*

> *(g) if the device is custom-made, the words 'custom-made device';*

> *(h) if the device is intended for clinical investigations, the words 'exclusively for clinical investigations ';*

> *(i) any special storage and/or handling conditions;*

161

(j) any special operating instructions;

(k) any warnings and/or precautions to take;

(l) year of manufacture for active devices other than those covered by (e). This indication maybe included in the batch or serial number;

(m) where applicable, method of sterilization;

(n) in the case of a device within the meaning of Article 1(4a), an indication that the device contains a human blood derivative.

13.4. If the intended purpose of the device is not obvious to the user, the manufacturer must clearly state it on the label and in the instructions for use.

13.5. Wherever reasonable and practicable, the devices and detachable components must be identified, where appropriate in terms of batches, to allow all appropriate action to detect any potential risk posed by the devices and detachable components.

13.6. Where appropriate, the instructions for use must contain the following particulars:

(a) the details referred to in Section 13.3, with the exception of (d) and (e);

(b) the performances referred to in Section 3 and any undesirable side- effects;

(c) if the device must be installed with or connected to other medical devices or equipment in order to operate as required for its intended purpose, sufficient details of its characteristics to identify the correct devices or equipment to use in order to obtain a safe combination;

(d) all the information needed to verify whether the device is properly installed and can operate correctly and safely, plus details of the nature and frequency of the maintenance and calibration needed to ensure that the devices operate properly and safely at all times;

(e) where appropriate, information to avoid certain risks in connection with implantation of the device;

(f) information regarding the risks of reciprocal interference posed by the presence of the device during specific investigations or treatment;

(g) the necessary instructions in the event of damage to the sterile packaging and, where appropriate, details of appropriate methods of re-sterilization;

(h) if the device is reusable, information on the appropriate processes to allow reuse, including cleaning, disinfection, packaging and, where appropriate, the method of sterilization of the device to be re-sterilized, and any restriction on the number of reuses.

Where devices are supplied with the intention that they be sterilized before use, the instructions for cleaning and sterilization must be such that, if correctly followed, the device will still comply with the requirements in Section I.

If the device bears an indication that the device is for single use, information on known characteristics and technical factors known to the manufacturer that could pose a risk if the device were to be re-used. If in accordance with Section 13.1 no instructions for use are needed, the information must be made available to the user upon request;

(i) details of any further treatment or handling needed before the device can be used (for example, sterilization, final assembly, etc.);

(j) in the case of devices emitting radiation for medical purposes, details of the nature, type, intensity and distribution of this radiation. The instructions for use must also include details allowing the medical staff to brief the patient on any contra-indications and any precautions to be taken. These details should cover in particular:

(k) precautions to be taken in the event of changes in the performance of the device;

(l) precautions to be taken as regards exposure, in reasonably foreseeable environmental conditions, to magnetic fields, external electrical influences, electrostatic discharge, pressure or variations in pressure, acceleration, thermal ignition sources, etc.;

(m) adequate information regarding the medicinal product or products which the device in question is designed to administer, including any limitations in the choice of substances to be delivered;

(n) precautions to be taken against any special, unusual risks related to the disposal of the device;

(o) medicinal substances, or human blood derivatives incorporated into the device as an integral part in accordance with Section 7.4;

(p) degree of accuracy claimed for devices with a measuring function;

(q) date of issue or the latest revision of the instructions for use.

What You Need to Know

Hopefully, you have had the chance to read the previous chapters in this book that were penned, actually typed, examining Articles 1 through 23. Several of the MDD Articles emphasize the importance of medical devices meeting their essential requirements. In fact, the need for a device to meet its essential requirements is one of the single-most important concepts device manufacturers need to understand. That being said, this chapter is all about understanding the importance of establishing essential requirements.

Annex I is divided into two major components, "*General Requirements*" and "*Requirements Regarding Design and Construction*." Many of the changes to the Directive that became effective on 21 March 2010 are nestled in Annex I. That being said, here is what device manufacturers need to know and understand.

1. Medical devices must be designed in such a way that they are safe and effective for their intended use. Device ergonomics shall be considered in an effort to reduce risk associated with the device user.

2. Identifying, understanding, and eliminating risk needs to be a key input into design, development, and manufacturing processes.

3. The finished medical device must achieve its performance objectives.

4. The finished medical device must work over its specified lifetime in its normal operating environment.

5. The device, including its packaging, must be designed to prevent damage during transportation and storage.

6. Undesirable side effects must be assessed for acceptable risk. It is Dr. D's experience that device designs that result in undesirable side effects being induced, should probably be redesigned to mitigate the risk.

7. A clinical evaluation is now required to support a device's conformity with these essential requirements. Just a quick note: if a manufacturer is trying to obtain approval for a Class III device in the EU, this is probably not going to

happen without a clinical trial.

8. Medical devices must be designed and manufactured taking into account their chemical, physical, and biological properties. In short, little things like toxicity, just kidding on the little things comment, must be considered. Device manufacturers need to ensure their devices are not poisoning the patient. That would be a bad thing. Additionally, devices must be designed and packaged to prevent contamination and residues to the person(s) transporting or storing the devices. Furthermore, if a device incorporates a medicinal product, the device must be verified against the requirements delineated within Annex I of Directive 2001/83/EC. If a medical device contains a human-blood derivative, the notified bodies will seek a scientific opinion from the European Medicines Agency (EMEA). Finally, devices that employ liquids in their use or remove liquids (fluids) from the body should not leak. The doctor classifies the "no-leak clause" as one of the proverbial no brainers associated with Medical Device Design-101. One additional thought, Dr. D was raised in the age of plastics and come to find out after all of the doctor's years on this planet, plasticizers are now considered bad things. Who knew? Maybe that is why Dr. D turned out this way. Regardless, device manufactures must now ensure devices, which employ phthalates as part of the device construction, be properly labeled with a warning. These phthalates must not come into contact with the blood path or be used to administer or remove liquids and medicines to and from the body.

9. Finished medical devices should not be a source for infection or microbial

contamination. In fact, if a device is delivered in a sterile state, the expectation is that the device should be sterile at the time of use. Imagine that, sterile devices should be sterile, thank you Dr. D. for such a brilliant and insightful comment.

10. If a device is intended to be used in conjunction with other devices, e.g., electrophysiological catheter and a radio-frequency generator, the device should work as advertised within that environment. If there are specific concerns or restrictions, these must be added to the device labeling. Some of the issues device manufacturers must consider are: electro-magnetic interference (EMI), magnetic fields, maintenance, calibration, material aging, and other risks associated with the environment in which a device is being used.

11. If a device performs or has a measuring function, the expectation is that the measurements made are accurate. There is an additional requirement that devices performing a measurement function express these measurements in legal limits. Can you say SI units?

12. European's tend to frown down upon devices that result in patients and users glowing in the dark. That being said, radiation levels must be reduced as much as practical, keeping in mind the intended use of the device. For devices intended to emit radiation, the devices must be fitted with a visual display or be able to produce an audible warning. Although Instructions for Use (IFU) are required for Class IIa, IIb, and III devices, additional instructions/warnings are required detailing the nature of the radiation being emitted and the

appropriate protective actions needing to be pursued. The same salient requirements hold true for devices emitting ionizing radiation, e.g., radiology equipment.

13. When the use of a medical device requires connection to a power source, the power supply/source must be designed in a way that ensures long-term reliability. If software is employed as an integral part of the power supply/source, the software must be validated. When a power supply's performance is linked directly to patient safety, an alarm or other signal device shall be present, to notify the user, a power failure has occurred. Other design considerations should include the operating environment; EMI, noise reduction, temperature, and electrical shorts resulting in electrical shock to the patient or user. Similar to having patients and healthcare professionals glowing in the dark due to exposure to radiation; shocking these same individuals with electricity is also considered a bad thing. Who knew?

14. Device manufacturers are required to delineate general product information and ensure this information ships with each devices. As a minimum, information such as; (a) selection information, (b) indications for use, (c) contraindications, (d) compatibility data, (e) warnings, (f) sterilization, (g) single-use, (h) batch code, (i) part number, (j) expiration date, (k) manufactured by, (l) manufacturing location, (m) handling, (n) storage, and any additional relevant information pertaining to the medical device, shall be considered. One final note, once this information is loaded onto a label or placed into the IFU, device manufacturers need to translate the information.

Why? Because Member States retain the right to have this information in their native tongue; and do not forget to save room for the CE Marking of Conformity.

What You Need to Do

Granted there is a whole bunch of information needing to be digested by device manufacturers in regards to meeting the essential requirements. The good news is the notified bodies are well-equipment to help device manufacturers navigate the Articles and Annexes collectively bundled under the MDD. The bad news is compliance is not an option. From Dr. D's perspective, the best advice the doctor can offer is to ensure essential requirements are considered starting at the conceptual phase of the design. Effectively planning for the essential requirements will result in a medical device that is safe and effective, with performance characteristics that conform to Annex I of the MDD.

Although all of the clauses associated with Annex I are important, device manufacturers need to focus on the labeling. Labeling is reviewed as part of the overall review and approval process (design dossiers and technical files); and Dr. D has witnessed the approval delays associated with incomplete or inaccurate labeling data, translation errors, and IFUs that are missing pages. Additionally, thanks to the advent of Prop 65 (thank you California) there has been an increased awareness in materials that can be categorized as carcinogens around the globe. The EU has jumped on this bandwagon and their efforts can be seen in the phthalate warning requirement added to Annex I in March of 2010. Finally, the re-use of single-use devices has become rampant in an effort for healthcare organizations to curtail skyrocketing healthcare costs. Now Dr. D <u>is not</u> a proponent of re-use; however, the practice is not going to go away. That being said, reprocessed medical devices are still required to meet their essential requirements.

Takeaways

A manufactured medical device's ability to meet essential requirements commences at the conceptual stage. All of the essential requirements must be considered as part of the design. A design and development process that results in shortcuts being taken, to improve on the speed-to-market, will result in a device manufacturer's failure to obtain approvals for market entry into the EU, or result in significant delays as the device goes through a redesign or errors and omissions to the labeling are corrected. When in doubt, work with your notified body. You pay the notified body, so they work for you. Yes the doctor knows that some notified bodies believe the relationship is the other way around; however a quick reminder as to who signs the checks should correct the relationship issue.

"Effectively planning for the essential requirements will result in a medical device that is safe and effective, with performance characteristics that conform to Annex I of the MDD."

Chapter 29 – *Annex II "EC Declaration of Conformity (full quality assurance system)"*

Chapter Twenty-nine – Annex II

Annex II (EC Declaration of Conformity – full quality assurance system) of Council

Directive 93/42/EEC, a.k.a., the Medical Device Directive (MDD) delineates the

regulatory requirements necessary for compliance with the Directive employing an

acceptable quality assurance system. Additionally, applications required by notified

bodies for the quality management system (QMS) and device review and approval are

included as part of Annex II. The good news is that for device manufacturers that already

comply with EN ISO 13485:2003, compliance with Annex II, from a QMS standpoint, is

a proverbial "cake walk." For device manufacturers not achieving compliance with the

EN ISO 13485:2003, compliance with Annex II is going to be problematic. In fact, you

might as well commence looking for another device market to enter because product

entry in to the European Union (EU) is not going to happen. Why - because device

manufacturers need a QMS approved by a notified body prior to making any application

for a device approval. Frankly speaking, entry into most markets will be problematic until

compliance is achieved. The bottom line for device manufacturers is in reality quite

simple. Having a documented and functional QMS is the price of admission into the

medical device market. As you read this chapter, please keep in mind that Dr. D is trying

to do more than just adumbrate (look-it-up) the information delineated within the MDD.

The doctor's goal is to provide insight into the interpretation and practical application of

the requirements.

The MDD – 93/42/EEC

ANNEX II – EC Declaration of Conformity (full quality assurance system)

*1. The manufacturer must ensure application of the quality system approved for the design,
manufacture and final inspection of the products concerned, as specified in Section 3 and is*

subject to audit as laid down in Sections 3.3 and 4 and to Community surveillance as specified in Section 5.

2. The EC declaration of conformity is the procedure whereby the manufacturer who fulfills the obligations imposed by Section 1 ensures and declares that the products concerned meet the provisions of this Directive which apply to them.

The manufacturer must affix the CE marking in accordance with Article 17 and draw up a written declaration of conformity. This declaration must cover one or more medical devices manufactured, clearly identified by means of product name, product code or other unambiguous reference and must be kept by the manufacturer.

*3. **Quality system***

3.1. The manufacturer must lodge an application for assessment of his quality system with a notified body. The application must include:

> *— the name and address of the manufacturer and any additional manufacturing site covered by the quality system,*

> *— all the relevant information on the product or product category covered by the procedure,*

> *— a written declaration that no application has been lodged with any other notified body for the same product-related quality system,* .

> *— the documentation on the quality system,*

> *— an undertaking by the manufacturer to fulfill the obligations imposed by the quality system approved,*

> *— an undertaking by the manufacturer to keep the approved quality system adequate and efficacious,*

> *— an undertaking by the manufacturer to institute and keep up to date a systematic procedure to review experience gained from devices in the post-production phase, including the provisions referred to in Annex X, and to implement appropriate means to apply any necessary corrective action. This undertaking must include an obligation for the manufacturer to notify the competent authorities of the following incidents immediately on learning of them:*
>> *(i)   any malfunction or deterioration in the characteristics and/or performance of a device, as well as any inadequacy in the instructions for use which might lead to or might have led to the death of a patient or user or to a serious deterioration in his state of health;*

>> *(ii)   (ii) any technical or medical reason connected with the characteristics or performance of a device leading for the reasons referred to in subparagraph (i) to systematic recall of devices of the same type by the manufacturer.*

3.2. Application of the quality system must ensure that the products conform to the provisions of this Directive which apply to them at every stage, from design to final inspection. All the elements, requirements and provisions adopted by the manufacturer for his quality system must be documented in a systematic and orderly manner in the form of written policies and procedures such as quality programs, quality plans, quality manuals and quality records.

It shall include in particular the corresponding documentation, data and records arising from the procedures referred to in point (c).

It shall include in particular an adequate description of:

(a) the manufacturer's quality objectives;

(b) the organization of the business and in particular:

— *the organizational structures, the responsibilities of the managerial staff and their organizational authority where quality of design and manufacture of the products is concerned,*

— *the methods of monitoring the efficient operation of the quality system and in particular its ability to achieve the desired quality of design and of product, including control of products which fail to conform,*

— *where the design, manufacture and/or final inspection and testing of the products, or elements thereof, is carried out by a third party, the methods of monitoring the efficient operation of the quality system and in particular the type and extent of control applied to the third party;*

(c) the procedures for monitoring and verifying the design of the products, including the corresponding documentation, and in particular:

— *a general description of the product, including any variants planned, and its intended use(s),*

— *the design specifications, including the standards which will be applied and the results of the risk analysis, and also a description of the solutions adopted to fulfill the essential requirements which apply to the products if the standards referred to in Article 5 are not applied in full,*

— *the techniques used to control and verify the design and the processes and systematic measures which will be used when the products are being designed,*

— *if the device is to be connected to other device(s) in order to operate as intended, proof must be provided that it conforms to the essential requirements when connected to any such device(s) having the characteristics specified by the manufacturer,*

— *a statement indicating whether or not the device incorporates, as an integral part, a substance or a human blood derivative referred to in section 7.4 of Annex I and the data on the tests conducted in this connection required to assess the safety, quality and usefulness of that substance or human blood derivative, taking account of the intended purpose of the device,*

— *a statement indicating whether or not the device is manufactured utilizing tissues of animal origin as referred to in Commission Directive 2003/32/EC (1),*

— *the solutions adopted as referred to in Annex I, Chapter I, Section 2,*

— *the pre-clinical evaluation,*

— *the clinical evaluation referred to in Annex X,*

— *the draft label and, where appropriate, instructions for use.*

(d) the inspection and quality assurance techniques at the manufacturing stage and in particular:

— *the processes and procedures which will be used, particularly as regards sterilization, purchasing and the relevant documents,*

— *the product identification procedures drawn up and kept up to date from drawings, specifications or other relevant documents at every stage of manufacture;*

(e) the appropriate tests and trials which will be carried out before, during and after manufacture, the frequency with which they will take place, and the test equipment used; it must be possible to trace back the calibration of the test equipment adequately.

3.3. The notified body must audit the quality system to determine whether it meets the requirements referred to in Section 3.2. It must presume that quality systems which implement the relevant harmonized standards conform to these requirements.

The assessment team must include at least one member with past experience of assessments of the technology concerned. The assessment procedure must include an assessment, on a representative basis, of the documentation of the design of the product(s) concerned, an inspection on the manufacturer's premises and, in duly substantiated cases, on the premises of the manufacturer's suppliers and/or subcontractors to inspect the manufacturing processes.

The decision is notified to the manufacturer. It must contain the conclusions of the inspection and a reasoned assessment.

3.4. The manufacturer must inform the notified body which approved the quality system of any plan for substantial changes to the quality system or the product-range covered. The notified body must assess the changes proposed and verify whether after these changes the quality system still meets the requirements referred to in Section 3.2. It must notify the manufacturer of its decision. This decision must contain the conclusions of the inspection and a reasoned assessment.

4. Examination of the design of the product

4.1. In addition to the obligations imposed by Section 3, the manufacturer must lodge with the notified body an application for examination of the design dossier relating to the product which he plans to manufacture and which falls into the category referred to in Section 3.1.

4.2. The application must describe the design, manufacture and performances of the product in question. It must include the documents needed to assess whether the product conforms to the requirements of this Directive, as referred to in Section 3.2 (c).

4.3. The notified body must examine the application and, if the product conforms to the relevant provisions of this Directive, issue the application with an EC design-examination certificate. The notified body may require the application to be completed by further tests or proof to allow assessment of conformity with the requirements of the Directive. The certificate must contain the conclusions of the examination, the conditions of validity, the data needed for identification of the approved design, where appropriate, a description of the intended purpose of the product.

In the case of devices referred to in Annex I, Section 7.4, second paragraph, the notified body shall, as regards the aspects referred to in that section, consult one of the competent authorities designated by the Member States in accordance with Directive 2001/83/EC or the EMEA before taking a decision. The opinion of the competent national authority or the EMEA must be drawn up within 210 days after receipt of valid documentation. The scientific opinion of the competent national authority or the EMEA must be included in the documentation concerning the device. The notified body will give due consideration to the views expressed in this consultation when making its decision. It will convey its final decision to the competent body concerned.

In the case of devices referred to in Annex I, Section 7.4, third paragraph, the scientific opinion of the EMEA must be included in the documentation concerning the device. The opinion of the EMEA must be drawn up within 210 days after receipt of valid documentation. The notified body will give due consideration to the opinion of the EMEA when making its decision. The notified body may not deliver the certificate if the EMEA's scientific opinion is unfavorable. It will convey its final decision to the EMEA.

In the case of devices manufactured utilizing tissues of animal origin as referred to in Directive 2003/32/EC, the notified body must follow the procedures referred to in that Directive.

4.4. Changes to the approved design must receive further approval from the notified body which issued the EC design-examination certificate wherever the changes could affect conformity with the essential requirements of the Directive or with the conditions prescribed for use of the product. The applicant shall inform the notified body which issued the EC design-examination certificate of any such changes made to the approved design. This additional approval must take the form of a supplement to the EC design- examination certificate.

*5. **Surveillance***

5.1. The aim of surveillance is to ensure that the manufacturer duly fulfills the obligations imposed by the approved quality system.

5.2. The manufacturer must authorize the notified body to carry out all the necessary inspections and supply it with all relevant information, in particular:

—   the documentation on the quality system,

— *the data stipulated in the part of the quality system relating to design, such as the results of analyses, calculations, tests, the solutions adopted as referred to in Annex I, Chapter I, Section 2, pre-clinical and clinical evaluation, post-market clinical follow-up plan and the results of the post-market clinical follow-up, if applicable, etc.,*

— *the data stipulated in the part of the quality system relating to manufacture, such as inspection reports and test data, calibration data, qualification reports of the personnel concerned, etc.*

5.3. The notified body must periodically carryout appropriate inspections and assessments to make sure that the manufacturer applies the approved quality system and must supply the manufacturer with an assessment report.

5.4. In addition, the notified body may pay unannounced visits to the manufacturer. At the time of such visits, the notified body may, where necessary, carryout or ask for tests in order to check that the quality system is working properly. It must provide the manufacturer with an inspection report and, if a test has been carried out, with a test report.

6. Administrative provisions

6.1. The manufacturer or his authorized representative must, for a period ending at least five years, and in the case of implantable devices at least 15 years, after the last product has been manufactured, keep at the disposal of the national authorities:

— *the declaration of conformity,*

— *the documentation referred to in the fourth indent of Section 3.1 and in particular the documentation, data and records referred to in the second paragraph of Section 3.2,*

— *the changes referred to in Section 3.4,*

— *the documentation referred to in Section 4.2, and*

— *the decisions and reports from the notified body as referred to in Sections 3.3, 4.3, 4.4, 5.3 and 5.4.*

7. Application to devices in Classes IIa and IIb.

7.1. In line with Article 11(2) and (3), this Annex may apply to products in Classes IIa and IIb. Section 4, however, does not apply.

7.2. For devices in Class IIa the notified body shall assess, as part of the assessment in Section 3.3, the technical documentation as described in Section3.2(c) for at least one representative sample for each device subcategory for compliance with the provisions of this Directive.

7.3. For devices in Class IIb the notified body shall assess, as part of the assessment in Section 3.3, the technical documentation as described in Section3.2(c) for at least one representative sample for each generic device group for compliance with the provisions of this Directive.

7.4. In choosing representative sample(s) the notified body shall take into account the novelty of the technology, similarities in design, technology, manufacturing and sterilization methods, the intended use and the results of any previous relevant assessments (e.g. with regard to physical, chemical or biological properties) that have been carried out in accordance with this Directive. The notified body shall document and keep available to the competent authority its rationale for the sample(s) taken.

7.5. Further samples shall be assessed by the notified body as part of the surveillance assessment referred to in Section 5.

8. *Application to the devices referred to Article 1(4a)*

Upon completing the manufacture of each batch of devices referred to in Article1(4a), the manufacturer shall inform the notified body of the release of the batch of devices and send to it the official certificate concerning the release of the batch of human blood derivative used in the device, issued by a State laboratory or a laboratory designated for that purpose by a Member State in accordance with Article 114(2) of Directive 2001/83/ EC.

What You Need to Know

The obvious "no-brainer" here is that a fully-functional QMS is a salient requirement for device manufacturers, period. Not unlike the FDA's Quality System Regulation (21 CFR, Part 820), Annex II requires that the QMS encompass more than just the routinely perceived elements associated with quality; such as inspection, measurement, CAPA, audits, nonconforming product, etc. In accordance with Annex II, QMS requirements begin with the design, continue with manufacturing, all the way through to final acceptance and distribution. In the last chapter, Dr. D explained the importance of devices meeting their essential requirements. Annex II supports the salient requirements associated with Annex I, by ensuring device manufacturers have an effective QMS, which in turn, supports the ability of a device to meet essential requirements.

The next point that needs to be made is that device manufacturers, as part of the application and approval process, are required to sign a declaration of conformity (DoC) that contains, as a minimum:

- Product name;

- Product code;

- First batch number manufacturer; and

- Other relevant information deemed important by the manufacturer.

Once the DoC has been prepared, do not forget to have the organization's Chief Jailable Office (CJO) sign and date the declaration. Make sure the CJO is aware of the consequences associated with signing a fraudulent document; and the lack of a fashion statement wearing an orange jump suit in the Netherlands makes. Once signed, now would be a good time to ensure that the CE marking of conformity, containing your notified body's registration number, is affixed to the product packaging.

Quality System

So where does this entire process begin, a.k.a. what came first, "the chicken or the egg?" In the case of the Directive, the QMS should always come first. The process commences with the device manufacturer making application to a notified body requesting the assessment of the quality system. As a minimum, the application shall include:

1. The name and address of the manufacturer and the manufacturing sites covered by the QMS;

2. Relevant product information;

3. A declaration that no other application exists (extremely important point as device manufacturers are permitted just one application per device in the EU – for additional clarification, a device manufacturer can have multiple notified bodies but cannot have the same device application with multiple notified

bodies);

4. QMS documentation;

5. The ongoing sustainment of the QMS by the device manufacturer; and

6. A post-market surveillance system to evaluate ongoing device performance characteristics.

Another salient point that device manufacturers need to know and understand reinforces bullet-point 5 depicted above. The QMS really does need to be fully functional from design to final acceptance inspection. Not so minor details such as procedures, written work instructions, quality plans, the quality manual, and all of the records collected are extremely important. In fact, one of the doctor's favorite mantras continues to be; "If it isn't documented in writing, it did not happen." That being said, a few of the key elements expected to be developed, in accordance with Annex II compliance and the application process, are:

1. Quality objectives;

2. Organizational structure, including roles and responsibilities of management;

3. Methods employed for QMS monitoring;

4. Procedures for monitoring and verifying design effectiveness;

5. Device interactions, when connected to other devices;

6. Statements delineating if human blood derivatives or tissues of animal origin have been used as part of the manufacturing process;

7. Clinical evaluation data;

8. A copy of the draft label and the instructions for use (IFU);

9. The application of inspection and quality assurance methodologies; and

10. Sterilization.

Once application has been made, the notified body will assess the QMS to ascertain if all of the requirements of the Directive have been fulfilled. If this is a device manufacturer's first time through the application and assessment process, Dr. D can safely state; "Expect to receive some minor deviations." Minor deviations will not prevent a device manufacturer from entering into the European device market, provided corrections to the QMS are expedited. However, if a major deviation is received, all bets are off. The major deviation will need to be corrected and effectiveness verified by the notified body prior to device entering into the EU.

Examination of the Design of the Product

Believe it or not, the application and approval of the QMS is, in Dr. D's humble opinion, the easy part of the equation. Device application and approval becomes the greater challenge. Once the QMS has been approved and the appropriate certificate issued by the notified body, application for the device can be made. In the good-ole-days, notified bodies only reviewed Class III device applications in great detail. Class IIa and IIb (exempt from Section 4 of Article II), were for the most part self-certified by the manufacturer, with the manufacturer claiming conformance to the essential requirements. This approach was clearly a two-edged sword with some manufacturers abusing the process by taking great liberties in claiming compliance to harmonized standards, where actual compliance was questionable. Regardless, as part of the application and examination process, the manufacturers must submit the design dossier (Class III devices) to their notified body for review and approval. The dossier shall contain sufficient granularity in regards to the device design, manufacturing, and performance characteristics. If the notified body, premised on their examination of the application and supporting data, believes the manufacturer and the device meet the required elements of the Directive, approval to market within the EU will be granted. Device manufacturers should not be surprised if this process takes several months, with multiple rounds of questions. Finally, once approval is granted, any changes impacting device conformity will need to be routed back to the notified body for review and approval.

Surveillance

Assuming a device manufacturer has obtained approval of their QMS, and their device application has been approved, now what? Is that the end of the process forever? Unfortunately, the answer would be a resounding no. The notified bodies are not very trusting, and by the way, they make significant coin through the performance of audits. That being said, surveillance audits now come into focus. Notified bodies perform surveillance audits with the aim of ensuring their clients (the device manufacturers) remain in compliance with the Directive. By the way, did the doctor mention they get paid for these activities? Device manufacturers can expect to host these surveillance visits annually, in between the actual full recertification audits. If the manufacturer is racking up a significant number of vigilance reports in the EU, they should expect more frequent visits.

Administrative Provisions

A device manufacturer cannot expect to play in the European medical device sandbox without administrative provisions. For example, a key provision of Annex II is the requirement that the device manufacturer or their European authorized representative must retain certain pieces of data for at least 5-years for medical devices and 15-years for implantable devices. As a minimum:

- The EU DoC;

- The design dossier or technical file;

- Device changes;

- Other relevant documentation; and

- Decisions and reports from their notified bodies;

must be retained and be made available upon request from the notified body or

Competent Authority.

Application to device in Classes IIa and IIb

I know Dr. D has presented, for the most part, examples supporting the

applicability of Annex II for Class III devices; however, the Annex does apply to Class

IIa and Class IIb as well. As stated earlier, Section 4 of Annex II <u>does not apply</u> for Class

IIa and Class IIb devices. Keep in mind, notified bodies are now requesting technical files

for review prior to granting approval for device entry into the EU. Additionally, notified

bodies are required to assess conformity of these products as part of their audits. During

their friendly visits, your notified bodies are required to pull at least once representative

sample from each device category. If a device manufacturer has a whole bunch of device

categories, they better be prepared to review a whole bunch of technical files with their

notified body. By the way, did Dr. D mention that the notified bodies get paid for these

activities?

Application of the Devices Referred to Article 1(4a)

Let Dr. D begin by refreshing the reader in regards to Article 1(4a) of the MDD.

Article 1(4a) is the clause that delineates requirements for medical devices that incorporate, as an integral part, a medicinal product derived from human blood. When a device falls into this category, Directive 2001/83/EC is applicable. The salient requirement associated with Annex II is the need for testing and certification issued by a State laboratory or an approved facility designated by a Member State.

What You Need to Do

So let us see if the doctor can break down Annex II into even smaller sound-bites device manufacturers need to know and apply (do). Yes, I know this can also be called Dr. D's broken-record time. For starters, device manufacturers need to make application to a notified body and have their QMS certified. The next step is for device manufacturers to make application with their notified body for their device(s) and seek review and approval (design dossier examination) for Class III devices. Device manufacturers can expect to pay for and receive surveillance audits. Device records shall be retained for a period of 5 or 15-years. Your notified body will assess conformance of Class IIa and IIb products as part of their audits. Finally, devices that incorporate human blood derivatives require additional testing and certification. Pretty simple stuff, right?

Takeaways

The takeaways from this chapter are eloquent in their simplicity. Annex II is really a straight forward document with requirements relatively easy to comprehend. In the gospel according to Dr. D, there are three major components; (a) application and approval of a QMS by a notified body; (b) application and approval of the actual device application by a notified body; and (c) retention of data for either 5 or 15-years, after the last device is placed onto the market, available upon request, by the notified body. If you can remember these three points, give yourselves an A. You just passed the Annex II test.

"Remember, in accordance with Annex II, QMS requirements begin with the design, continue with manufacturing."

Chapter 30 – *Annex III "EC-Type Examination"*

Chapter Thirty – Annex III

Annex III (EC Type - Examination) of Council Directive 93/42/EEC, a.k.a., the Medical Device Directive (MDD) delineates the requirements for having one's head examined in the European Union (EU). In short, the Annex III requirement clearly states that one must definitely have their head examined if they choose to work in quality or regulatory in the medical device industry. Ha, ha, ha, I hope Dr. D has captured your attention with my attempt at some levity. All kidding aside, there is an examination associated with the Annex III requirement; however, it deals with a medical device manufacturer's notified body and the examination of their device application and technical data for entry into the EU's medical device market. The doctor's experience in regard to the application submission and review process just might lead some device industry professionals to form the conclusion that maybe having one's head examined might not be too far off base. Regardless, this Annex is a salient requirement of the Directive. Not unlike the game of Monopoly, where one must "pass go to collect $200.00," notified bodies will not issue an EC Type Examination Certificate if device manufacturers are not able to "pass the device examination process." Simply put, no certificate equates to no sales; a.k.a., no revenue stream coming from the European market. By now, I hope the readers of Dr. D's second book realize that although Dr. D lays no claim to being an overly sagacious (look-it-up) disciple of medical device regulations, my belief in compliance is driven by the underlying principle that medical devices must be safe and effective, regardless of market.

The MDD – 93/42/EEC

ANNEX III – EC Type - Examination

1. EC type-examination is the procedure whereby a notified body ascertains and certifies that a representative sample of the production covered fulfills the relevant provisions of this Directive.

2. The application includes:

> *— the name and address of the manufacturer and the name and address of the authorized representative if the application is lodged by the representative,*

> *— the documentation described in Section 3 needed to assess the conformity of the representative sample of the production in question, hereinafter referred to as the 'type', with the requirements of this Directive. The applicant must make a 'type' available to the notified body. The notified body may request other samples as necessary,*

> *— a written declaration that no application has been lodged with any other notified body for the same type.*

3. The documentation must allow an understanding of the design, the manufacture and the performances of the product and must contain the following items in particular:

> *— a general description of the type, including any variants planned, and its intended use(s),*

> *— design drawings, methods of manufacture envisaged, in particular as regards sterilization, and diagrams of components, sub-assemblies, circuits, etc.,*

> *— the descriptions and explanations necessary to understand the above- mentioned drawings and diagrams and the operation of the product,*

> *— a list of the standards referred to in Article 5, applied in full or in part, and descriptions of the solutions adopted to meet the essential requirements if the standards referred to in Article 5 have not been applied in full,*

> *— the results of the design calculations, risk analysis, investigations, technical tests, etc. carried out,*

> *— a statement indicating whether or not the device incorporates, as an integral part, a substance, or human blood derivative, referred to in Section7.4 of Annex I, and the data on the tests conducted in this connection which are required to assess the safety, quality and usefulness of that substance, or human blood derivative, taking account of the intended purpose of the device,*

> *— a statement indicating whether or not the device is manufactured utilizing tissues of animal origin as referred to in Directive 2003/32/EC,*

> *— the solutions adopted as referred to in Annex I, Chapter I, Section 2,*

> *— the preclinical evaluation, —the clinical evaluation referred to in Annex X,*

> *— the draft label and, where appropriate, instructions for use.*

4. The notified body must:

4.1. examine and assess the documentation and verify that the type has been manufactured inconformity with that documentation; it must also record the items designed inconformity with the applicable provisions of the standards referred to in Article 5, as well as the items not designed on the basis of the relevant provisions of the above mentioned standards;

4.2. carryout or arrange for the appropriate inspections and the tests necessary to verify whether the solutions adopted by the manufacturer meet the essential requirements of this Directive if the standards referred to in Article 5 have not been applied; if the device is to be connected to other device(s) in order to operate as intended, proof must be provided that it conforms to the essential requirements when connected to any such device (s) having the characteristics specified by the manufacturer;

4.3. carry out or arrange for the appropriate inspections and the tests necessary to verify whether, if the manufacturer has chosen to apply the relevant standards, these have actually been applied;

4.4. agree with the applicant on the place where the necessary inspections and tests will be carried out.

5. If the type conforms to the provisions of this Directive, the notified body issues the applicant with an EC type-examination certificate. The certificate must contain the name and address of the manufacturer, the conclusions of the inspection, the conditions of validity and the data needed for identification of the type approved. The relevant parts of the documentation must be annexed to the certificate and a copy kept by the notified body.

In the case of devices referred to in Annex I, Section 7.4, second paragraph, the notified body shall, as regards the aspects referred to in that section, consult one of the authorities designated by the Member States in accordance with Directive 2001/83/EC or the EMEA before taking a decision. The opinion of the competent national authority or the EMEA must be drawn up within 210 days after receipt of valid documentation. The scientific opinion of the competent national authority or the EMEA must be included in the documentation concerning the device. The notified body will give due consideration to the views expressed in this consultation when making its decision. It will convey its final decision to the competent body concerned.

In the case of devices referred to in Annex I, Section 7.4, third paragraph, the scientific opinion of the EMEA must be included in the documentation concerning the device. The opinion of the EMEA must be drawn up within 210 days after receipt of valid documentation. The notified body will give due consideration to the opinion of the EMEA when making its decision. The notified body may not deliver the certificate if the EMEA's scientific opinion is unfavorable. It will convey its final decision to the EMEA.

In the case of devices manufactured utilizing tissues of animal origin as referred to in Directive 2003/32/EC, the notified body must follow the procedures referred to in that Directive.

6. The applicant must inform the notified body which issued the EC type-examination certificate of any significant change made to the approved product. Changes to the approved product must receive further approval from the notified body which issued the EC type-examination certificate wherever the changes may affect conformity with the essential requirements or with the conditions prescribed for use of the product. This new approval must, where appropriate, take the form of a supplement to the initial EC type-examination certificate.

7. *Administrative provisions*

7.2. Other notified bodies may obtain a copy of the EC type-examination certificates and/or the supplements thereto. The Annexes to the certificates must be made available to other notified bodies on reasoned application, after the manufacturer has been informed.

7.3. The manufacturer or his authorized representative must keep with the technical documentation copies of EC type-examination certificates and their additions for a period ending at least five years after the last device has been manufactured. In the case of implantable devices, the period shall beat least 15years after the last product has been manufactured.

What You Need to Know

Since the EC Type – Examination is so dependent on the notified bodies, device manufacturers need to select a notified body they are comfortable working with, which should include familiarity with the manufacturer's device technology. That being said, Annex III is all about the notified bodies and their authority to review and certify products. Under the requirements of Annex III, the device manufacturer must file an application and provide relevant device technical information (design dossier) to their notified body for review. As a minimum, the application shall include:

1. The manufacturer's name and address;

2. The name and address of their European authorized representative;

3. The appropriate technical documentation (design dossier); and

4. A written declaration that clearly states that a similar application has not been filed with another notified body. Remember, only one device application, for each device type, is permitted in the EU.

Documentation

The documentation will vary depending on the medical device being submitted for review. For example, if a device incorporates a human blood derivative, additional testing will be required. In general, the following pieces of information will need to be incorporated into the technical documentation:

1. Device description, including variations of the device that are being planned (a.k.a., product-line extensions);

2. The intended use of the device;

3. Device design drawings (including component drawings);

4. Manufacturing / production drawings;

5. Method of sterilization;

6. A list of applicable standards employed (hopefully, European Harmonized Standards);

7. The results of design and development activities, including testing performed;

8. The application of risk analysis tools;

9. A statement indicating the presence, or lack of, human blood derivatives;

10. A statement indication the presence, or lack of, animal tissues;

11. Pre-clinical and clinical evaluations performed; and

12. A copy of the device's draft label and instructions for use, containing English and 135 languages and dialects (just kidding about the 135; however, translation for applicable languages spoken within the EU, minus the dialects will be required for product distribution within non-English speaking Member States).

Notified Body Requirements

Under the requirements delineated within Annex III, the notified bodies are required to make their clients miserable by rejecting applications multiple times and by asking silly questions that have intuitively obvious answers to the most casual observers. Sorry, if Dr. D has a jaded view of this process; however, the doctor has experienced

"The Good, The Bad, and The Ugly" – great movie – when working with notified bodies and their review of technical data. That being said, the notified bodies are required to:

1. Exam the technical documentation and verify that the manufactured medical device is in conformance with its specifications and standards claimed;

2. Arrange for inspections and testing, as applicable, to verify device conformance to essential requirements;

3. Arrange for inspection and testing to ascertain correct selection and use of standards, chosen by the manufacturer;

4. Work in conjunction with the device manufacturer in selecting an appropriate location for additional inspection and test, if deemed necessary and appropriate; and

5. Issue a certification upon the successful review and acceptance of the application and technical documentation.

Device Manufacturer (a.k.a., the applicant)

Once the device manufacturer receives the certificate of examination, the overall process does not end. In fact, as long as the approved medical device remains on the European market and for a time after the device is no longer available on the market; there will always be additional requirements needing to be met. One of the more salient requirements is the need to submit all proposed device changes, deemed as significant, to the notified body for review and approval. What is the heck does "significant change" mean Dr. D? The doctor likes to categorize "significant change" as a change that influences device form, fit, function, or performance against the originally approved product specification. When in doubt, play it safe and ask your notified body for guidance. Not unlike the submission of a Class III device change in the United States, where a 30-day PMA supplement is required by the FDA, the same concept holds true for the EU.

Administrative Provisions

Two key provisions associated with Annex III relate to the rights of other notified bodies to obtain copies of examination certificates and the retention of examination certificates. (1) Other notified bodies may request a copy of any examination certification and their additions, by making a formal request through application. If the reason depicted is deemed reasonable, a copy of the examination certificate will be supplied, after the manufacturer has been notified. (2) The retention period for examination certificates will be a minimum of 5-years (after last device is manufactured) or 15-years for implantable devices. The device manufacturer or the device manufacturer's EU authorized representative shall be tasked in retaining these copies.

What You Need to Do

The single-most important thing that device manufacturers need to do is prepare a design dossier that is clear, concise, and complete. Early in this chapter, the doctor poked fun at notified bodies and their notoriously painful review process. Device manufactures can easily fall prey to the infinite "do-loop" if key components of the dossier are missing. Believe it or not, leaving out little things like sterilization, shelf-life testing, and package-integrity testing can result in significant delays to the approval process.

Additionally, not unlike the FDA, notified bodies do not like surprises. Yes, the notified bodies work for the device manufacturers; and the device manufacturers pay for this service. The service provided is not cheap. Remember, protracted reviews due to the inadvertent omission of technical data equates to more money being spent as a result. One more thing to remember is the potential for revenue lost as a device application remains in limbo due to an incomplete design dossier or errors in technical documentation. These problematic issues force the notified body's reviewer to play a game of 50-questions. It is just not worth the pain not to get the submission right the first time. Will there be questions surrounding the submission? Absolutely, but the hope is that the amount of questions generated are just a handful needing to address minor details.

Finally, never forget about the need to retain the examination certificate and the technical documentation (a.k.a., the design dossier) for the required length of time. The doctor has experienced on a couple of occasions requests for the dossier being made by a Competent Authority, shortly after device production has officially stopped.

Takeaways

For this chapter, there are just two takeaways device manufacturers need to clearly understand and remember. The application process begins with a device application supported by a clear, concise, and complete design dossier. Device manufacturers want to ensure all of the technical documentation is readily available for their notified bodies during the examination process. A poorly constructed and/or incomplete design dossier will result in an initial rejection, the proverbial game of "50-questions" and a protracted review and approval process, keeping the device out of the European market. The second takeaway is the responsibilities associated with certificate and data retention. Just because a device manufacturer stops manufacturing a device does not mean it is ok to toss out the certificates or design dossier. There is a mandatory retention period of either 5 or 15-years, depending on the application of the device.

"Medical devices must be safe and effective, regardless of market"

Chapter 31 – *Annex IV "EC Verification"*

Chapter Thirty-one – Annex IV

Annex IV (EC Verification) of Council Directive 93/42/EEC, a.k.a., the Medical Device Directive (MDD) delineates the requirements for the verification of a medical device company's checking-account balance prior to a notified body accepting a contract. Ha, ha, ha, just like the previous chapter, Dr. D thought he would inject some levity into a topic often deemed boring. Now that the doctor has finally stopped laughing, there is a verification process associated with the Annex IV. It is a criminal background check to verify a device manufacturer's Chief Jailable Officer (CJO) has never been incarcerated in The Hague, ha, ha, ha, etc. Alright, the doctor promises to stop. Seriously, Annex IV involves a whole bunch of trust as device manufacturers are expected to self-test and self-verify their devices meet essential requirements. Not too long ago, this process equated to the proverbial "free pass" for device manufacturers; however, today, not so much. As part of the revamped MDD, notified bodies are required to sample and exam technical files (Class IIa and IIb devices) from each product family a device manufacturer sells into the EU, during the annual audit performed by notified bodies. Additionally, Dr. D is now seeing that notified bodies are asking to review technical files prior to device manufacturers being given permission to affix the CE Marking of Conformity. Since the doctor has witnessed "The Good, The Bad, and The Ugly" (Dr. D loved this movie so he apologizes for his ongoing reference to it – but it is the doctor's book) when it comes to the completeness of technical files; the additional oversight by notified bodies is a good thing. Remember, Dr. D will never knowingly lead the readers astray, but always attempt to present his somewhat colorful perception of the irrefragable (look-it-up) truth surrounding regulatory compliance.

The MDD – 93/42/EEC

ANNEX IV – EC Verification

1. EC verification is the procedure whereby the manufacturer or his authorized representative ensures and declares that the products which have been subject to the procedure set out in Section 4 conform to the type described in the EC type-examination certificate and meet the requirements of this Directive which apply to them.

2. The manufacturer must take all the measures necessary to ensure that the manufacturing process produces products which conform to the type described in the EC type-examination certificate and to the requirements of the Directive which apply to them. Before the start of manufacture, the manufacturer must prepare documents defining the manufacturing process, in particular as regards sterilization where necessary, together with all the routine, pre-established provisions to be implemented to ensure homogeneous production and, where appropriate, conformity of the products with the type described in the EC type-examination certificate and with the requirements of this Directive which apply to them. The manufacturer must affix the CE marking in accordance with Article 17 and draw up a declaration of conformity.

In addition, for products placed on the market in sterile condition, and only for those aspects of the manufacturing process designed to secure and maintain sterility, the manufacturer must apply the provisions of Annex V, Sections3 and 4.

3. The manufacturer must undertake to institute and keep up to date a systematic procedure to review experience gained from devices in the post-production phase, including the provisions referred to in Annex X, and to implement appropriate means to apply any necessary corrective action. This undertaking must include an obligation for the manufacturer to notify the competent authorities of the following incidents immediately on learning of them:

(i)   any malfunction or deterioration in the characteristics and/or performance of a device, as well as any inadequacy in the labeling or the instructions for use which might lead to or might have led to the death of a patient or user or to a serious deterioration in his state of health;

(ii)   any technical or medical reason connected with the characteristics or performance of a device for the reasons referred to in subparagraph (i) leading to systematic recall of devices of the same type by the manufacturer.

4. The notified body must carry out the appropriate examinations and tests in order to verify the conformity of the product with the requirements of the Directive either by examining and testing every product as specified in Section 5 or by examining and testing products on a statistical basis as specified in Section 6, as the manufacturer decides.

The aforementioned checks do not apply to those aspects of the manufacturing process designed to secure sterility.

5. Verification by examination and testing of every product

5.1. Every product is examined individually and the appropriate tests defined in the relevant standard(s) referred to in Article 5 or equivalent tests must be carried out in order to verify, where appropriate, the conformity of the products with the EC type described in the type-examination certificate and with the requirements of the Directive which apply to them.

5.2. The notified body must affix, or have affixed its identification number to each approved product and must draw up a written certificate of conformity relating to the tests carried out.

6. *Statistical verification*

6.1. The manufacturer must present the manufactured products in the form of homogeneous batches.

6.2. A random sample is taken from each batch. The products which makeup the sample are examined individually and the appropriate tests defined in the relevant standard(s) referred to in Article 5 or equivalent tests must be carried out to verify, where appropriate, the conformity of the products with the type described in the EC type-examination certificate and with the requirements of the Directive which apply to them in order to determine whether to accept or reject the batch.

6.3. Statistical control of products will be based on attributes and/or variables, entailing sampling schemes with operational characteristics which ensure a high level of safety and performance according to the state of the art. The sampling schemes will be established by the harmonized standards referred to in Article 5, taking account of the specific nature of the product categories in question.

6.4. If the batch is accepted, the notified body affixes or has affixed its identification number to each product and draws up a written certificate of conformity relating to the tests carried out. All products in the batch maybe put on the market except any in the sample which failed to conform.

If a batch is rejected, the competent notified body must take appropriate measures to prevent the batch from being placed on the market. In the event of frequent rejection of batches, the notified body may suspend the statistical verification.

The manufacturer may, on the responsibility of the notified body, affix the notified body's identification number during the manufacturing process.

7. *Administrative provisions*

The manufacturer or his authorized representative must, for a period ending at least five years, and in the case of implantable devices at least 15 years, after the last product has been manufactured, make available to the national authorities:

— *the declaration of conformity,*

— *the documentation referred to in Section 2,*

— *the certificates referred to in Sections 5.2 and 6.4,*

— *where appropriate, the type-examination certificate referred to in Annex III.*

8. *Application to devices in Class IIa*

In line with Article 11 (2), this Annex may apply to products in Class IIa, subject to the following:

8.1. in derogation from Sections 1 and 2, by virtue of the declaration of conformity the manufacturer ensures and declares that the products in Class IIa are manufactured inconformity with the technical documentation referred to in Section 3 of Annex VII and meet the requirements of this Directive which apply to them;

8.2. in derogation from Sections 1, 2, 5 and 6, the verifications conducted by the notified body are intended to confirm the conformity of the products in Class IIa with the technical documentation referred to in Section 3 of Annex VII.

*9. **Application to devices referred to in Article 1(4a)***

In the case of section 5, upon completing the manufacture of each batch of devices referred to in Article 1(4a), and in the case of verification under section6, the manufacturer shall inform the notified body of the release of this batch of devices and send to it the official certificate concerning the release of the batch of human blood derivative used in the device issued by a State laboratory or a laboratory designated for that purpose by a Member State in accordance with Article 114(2) of Directive 2001/83/ EC.

What You Need to Know

Dr. D views Annex IV of the Directive as being broken down into six salient elements. Remember, the premise of this Annex is the device manufacturer's ability to verify and declare that their product meets the requirements of the MDD, as applicable. Additionally, the notified bodies are required to exam and test product, on a sample basis as a minimum, prior to allowing the affixing of the CE Mark to a manufacturer's product.

Element One – As previously stated, the device manufacturer or their European Authorized Representative has the authority to exam, verify, and declare their product (Class IIa and IIb) meets the Directive, as applicable. As part of this process, the manufacturer must ensure all of the appropriate steps have been taken in regards to documenting the design and development, verification activities, validation activities, testing, including the entire manufacturing process and sterilization. In reality, the technical file, once assembled, will look like a design dossier (Class III device). Prior to the first production device being manufactured, the device manufacturer must draw up the Declaration of Conformity, ensure that it is signed by the CJO, and send the Declaration to their notified body for review and approval. Once approved, the CE Mark can be affixed to the product. Just an FYI – chances are pretty good that the notified body is going to want to see the technical file, as well. So device manufacturers need to ensure the technical file is robust; and contains technical data supporting claims of compliance with essential requirements.

Element Two – Post-market surveillance activities, just like the United States, are applicable for the EU as well. Device manufacturers are expected to collect product performance issues, including adverse events and use this information to correct product deficiencies. Device manufacturers are required to notify the Competent Authorities when: (a) device malfunctions; (b) device performance deterioration; (c) device labeling issues; or (d) device instructions for use issues; have resulted in serious injury to, or death of a patient or user. Product recalls, driven by the same reasons just given, also require notification to the Competent Authorities. Trust Dr. D when I say, "If a device manufacturer's products are racking up a significant number of vigilant reports in the EU, they can expect a telephone call and a visit from their notified body."

Element Three – As previously stated, the notified bodies are required to test and exam devices that were previously self-verified by the manufacturer. In pursuing this objective, notified bodies have two options; (a) 100 percent examination and test (minus sterilization); and (b) sample examination and test. Regardless, device manufacturers can expect some level of verification by their notified bodies. Remember, as a result of changes made to the MDD, there are no more free passes.

Element Four – The manufacturer or the manufacturer's authorized rep is required to retain data associated with this Annex for a period of 5-years or 15-years (implantable). As a minimum, this data shall include:

1. The Declaration of Conformity;

2. Relevant documentation;

3. Certificates; and

4. The type-examination certificate, as appropriate.

Element Five – Is an applicability and derogation clause for Class IIa devices. As a device manufacturer, if you have been creating robust technical files for all of your Class IIa and IIb devices, including accessory technical data files, you should have no worries in regards to compliance with the Annex IV. As Dr. D stated earlier, notified bodies are now required to exam a sample of technical files from each product category during the annual audits. One additional note – the doctor has experienced the pain of having to correct and revise technical files that resided on a shelf for several years without any review or updates, including simple tasks like blowing the dust off the cover of a file. Technical files are dynamic documents requiring routine reviews and updates. Remember, if testing was performed to a harmonized standard, and that standard has changed, the technical file and applicable data must be reviewed for ongoing compliance to that change. If additional testing is required to claim compliance, manufacturers must generate the protocol and perform the testing. This is not an option but should be considered a salient requirement of the Directive.

Element Six – Is the human blood derivative clause. If a medical device contains a human blood derivative, additional testing is required by a State laboratory or other approved testing laboratory specified by a Member State.

What You Need to Do

Chapter after chapter, the doctor preaches about the importance of compliance to regulations. Dr. D's ongoing message is that compliance counts. That being said, performing device testing, executing effective verification and validation activities, and considering the influence and need to comply with applicable harmonized standards, each form a part of the foundation for a robust technical file. Device manufacturers need to concentrate on developing a robust technical file to facilitate the introduction of Class IIa and Class IIb product into the European device market. In fact, Dr. D strongly suggests creating a Standard Operating Procedure (SOP) dedicated specifically to the creation and management of technical files. This SOP should also contain a template that supports the standardization of an acceptable technical file format. The notified bodies love standardization as it makes their job easier when it comes to reviews. Remember, device manufacturers pay the notified bodies for their time and service. Call the doctor crazy but a reduction in hours expended by the notified body should equate to fewer dollars, pesos, or euros being spent by manufacturers.

Takeaways

For this chapter, Dr. D will leave the readers with three takeaways. (1) Device manufacturers are empowered by Annex IV to exam, verify, and certify that their product meets essential requirements and the Directive. (2) Notified bodies are required to keep the device manufacturers honest by performing examination and verification activities to ensure product does in fact meet essential requirements and the Directive. (3) If a device manufacturer's product is deemed to be less than safe and effective and causing harm and/or death to the patient or user, these events must be reported to the Competent

Authorities. Finally, device manufacturers can expect a visit from their notified body if their products are racking up the vigilant reports in the EU.

In reality, the technical file, once assembled, will look like a design dossier (Class III device).

Chapter 32 – *Annex V "EC Declaration of Conformity – Production Quality System"*

Chapter Thirty-two – Annex V

Annex V (*EC Declaration of Conformity – Production Quality Assurance*) of Council

Directive 93/42/EEC, a.k.a., the Medical Device Directive (MDD) delineates the

requirements for device manufacturers and their need to employ an approved quality

system in support of manufacturing and inspection. Wait a minute, having an approved-

quality system is a fundamental requirement for entrance into the European device

market? Who knew? I know – please stop being so darned facetious Dr. D. One thing the

doctor has learned from playing in the medical device industry sandbox is the variegated

(look-it-up) interpretations of mandated regulations governing an already heavily

regulated industry. At times, the MDD can be perceived as one of those propitious (look-

it-up) pieces of regulation. Regardless, the MDD equates to law within the EU; and

device manufacturers are required to comply with the MDD. Dr. D would like to reiterate

DG Rule # 1 - Compliance to regulations is not optional, it is mandatory and dictated by

law. That being said, Annex V is similar in construction to Annex II, minus the mention

of the design component. Three of the salient components of Annex V, that will be

discussed in this chapter, are: (a) device manufacturers must have an approved quality

system; (b) device manufacturers must create and submit an EC Declaration of

Conformity to their notified body; and (c) device manufacturers must affix the CE

Marking, that reflects their notified body's registration number to all product approved

for importation into and distribution within the EU.

The MDD – 93/42/EEC

ANNEX V – EC Declaration of Conformity – Production Quality System

1. The manufacturer must ensure application of the quality system approved for the manufacture of the products concerned and carryout the final inspection, as specified in Section 3, and is subject to the Community surveillance referred to in Section 4.

2. The EC declaration of conformity is the part of the procedure whereby the manufacturer who fulfills the obligations imposed by Section 1 ensures and declares that the products concerned conform to the type described in the EC type-examination certificate and meet the provisions of this Directive which apply to them.

The manufacturer must affix the CE marking in accordance with Article 17 and draw up a written declaration of conformity. This declaration must cover one or more medical devices manufactured, clearly identified by means of product name, product code or other unambiguous reference, and must be kept by the manufacturer.

Quality system

3.1. The manufacturer must lodge an application for assessment of his quality system with a notified body.

The application must include:

— *the name and address of the manufacturer,*

— *all the relevant information on the product or product category covered by the procedure,*

— *a written declaration that no application has been lodged with any other notified body for the same products,*

— *the documentation on the quality system,*

— *an undertaking to fulfill the obligations imposed by the quality system is approved,*

— *an undertaking to maintain the practicability and effectiveness of the approved quality system,*

— *where appropriate, the technical documentation on the types approved and a copy of the EC type-examination certificates,*

— *an undertaking by the manufacturer to institute and keep up to date a systematic procedure to review experience gained from devices in the post-production phase, including the provisions referred to in Annex X, and to implement appropriate means to apply any necessary corrective action. This undertaking must include an obligation for the manufacturer to notify the competent authorities of the following incidents immediately on learning of them:*

    (i)   any malfunction or deterioration in the characteristics and/or performance of a device, as well as any inadequacy in the labeling or the instructions for use which might lead to or might have led to the death of a patient or user or to a serious deterioration in his state of health;

    (ii)   any technical or medical reason connected with the characteristics or performance of a device for the reasons referred to in subparagraph (i)

above leading to a systematic recall of devices of the same type by the manufacturer.

3.2. Application of the quality system must ensure that the products conform to the type described in the EC type-examination certificate.

All the elements, requirements and provisions adopted by the manufacturer for his quality system must be documented in a systematic and orderly manner in the form of written policy statements and procedures. This quality system documentation must permit uniform interpretation of the quality policy and procedures such as quality programs, plans, manuals and records.

It must include in particular an adequate description of:

(a) the manufacturer's quality objectives;

(b) the organization of the business and in particular:

— the organizational structures, the responsibilities of the managerial staff and their organizational authority where manufacture of the products is concerned,

— the methods of monitoring the efficient operation of the quality system and in particular its ability to achieve the desired quality of product, including control of products which fail to conform,

— where the manufacture and/or final inspection and testing of the products, or elements thereof, are carried out by a third party, the methods of monitoring the efficient operation of the quality system and in particular the type and extent of control applied to the third party;

(c) the inspection and quality assurance techniques at the manufacturing stage and in particular:

— the processes and procedures which will be used, particularly as regards sterilization, purchasing and the relevant documents,

— the product identification procedures drawn up and kept up to date from drawings, specifications or other relevant documents at every stage of manufacture;

(d) the appropriate tests and trials to be carried out before, during and after manufacture, the frequency with which they will take place, and the test equipment used; it must be possible adequately to trace back the calibration of the test equipment.

3.3. The notified body must audit the quality system to determine whether it meets the requirements referred to in Section 3.2. It must presume that quality systems which implement the relevant harmonized standards conform to these requirements.

The assessment team must include at least one member with past experience of assessments of the technology concerned. The assessment procedure must include an inspection on the manufacturer's premises and, in duly substantiated cases, on the premises of the manufacturer's suppliers to inspect the manufacturing processes.

The decision must be notified to the manufacturer after the final inspection and contain the conclusions of the inspection and a reasoned assessment.

3.4. The manufacturer must inform the notified body which approved the quality system of any plan for substantial changes to the quality system.

The notified body must assess the changes proposed and verify whether after these changes the quality system still meets the requirements referred to in Section 3.2.

After the abovementioned information has been received the decision is notified to the manufacturer. It must contain the conclusions of the inspection and a reasoned assessment.

*4. **Surveillance***

4.1. The aim of surveillance is to ensure that the manufacturer duly fulfills the obligations imposed by the approved quality system.

4.2. The manufacturer authorizes the notified body to carry out all the necessary inspections and must supply it with all relevant information, in particular:

> *— the documentation on the quality system,*

> *— the technical documentation,*

> *— the data stipulated in the part of the quality system relating to manufacture, such as inspection reports and test data, calibration data, qualification reports of the personnel concerned, etc.*

4.3. The notified body must periodically carryout appropriate inspections and assessments to make sure that the manufacturer applies the approved quality system and supply the manufacturer with an assessment report.

4.4. In addition, the notified body may pay unannounced visits to the manufacturer. At the time of such visits, the notified body may, where necessary, carryout or ask for tests in order to check that the quality system is working properly. It must provide the manufacturer with an inspection report and, if a test has been carried out, with a test report.

*5. **Administrative provisions***

5.1. The manufacturer or his authorized representative must, for a period ending at least five years, and in the case of implantable devices at least 15 years, after the last product has been manufactured, make available to the national authorities:

> *— the declaration of conformity,*

> *— the documentation referred to in the fourth indent of Section 3.1,*

> *— the changes referred to in Section 3.4,*

> *— the documentation referred to in the seventh indent of Section 3.1,*

— the decisions and reports from the notified body as referred to in Sections 4.3 and 4.4,

— where appropriate, the type-examination certificate referred to in Annex III.

6. Application to devices in Class IIa In line with Article 11(2), this Annex may apply to products in Class IIa, subject to the following:

6.1. By way of derogation from Sections 2, 3.1 and 3.2, by virtue of the declaration of conformity the manufacturer ensures and declares that the products in Class IIa are manufactured inconformity with the technical documentation referred to in Section 3 of Annex VII and meet the requirements of this Directive which apply to them.

6.2. For devices in Class IIa the notified body shall assess, as part of the assessment in Section 3.3, the technical documentation as described in Section 3 of Annex VII for at least one representative sample for each device subcategory for compliance with the provisions of this Directive.

6.3. In choosing representative sample(s) the notified body shall take into account the novelty of the technology, similarities in design, technology, manufacturing and sterilization methods, the intended use and the results of any previous relevant assessments (e.g. with regard to physical, chemical or biological properties) that have been carried out in accordance with this Directive. The notified body shall document and keep available to the competent authority its rationale for the sample(s) taken.

6.4. Further samples shall be assessed by the notified body as part of the surveillance assessment referred to in Section 4.3.

7. Application to devices referred to in Article 1(4a) Upon completing the manufacture of each batch of devices referred to in Article 1(4a), the manufacturer shall inform the notified body of the release of the batch of devices and send to it the official certificate concerning the release of the batch of human blood derivative used in the device issued by a State laboratory or a laboratory designated for that purpose by a Member State in accordance with Article 114(2) of Directive 2001/83/ EC.

What You Need to Know

Let Dr. D start by reiterating three salient requirements depicting in the introduction. Broken-record time, device manufactures must have an approved quality system, an EC Declaration of Conformity signed by the Chief Jailable Officer (CJO), and CE Marks affixed to products, but wait there's more (sounds like a commercial). A notified body does not just fall from the sky. Device manufacturers must go out and select one; and before the doctor forgets, this process costs money or should Dr. D say,

"Euros." There are some extremely competent notified bodies out there. The doctor has worked with TUV-R, BSI, DEKRA, TUV-SUD, GMED, and NSAI (Dr. D is not a paid spokesperson for these firms). I recommend selecting one that has familiarity with your products; and your organization is comfortable working with for the duration. This will be a long-term relationship so choose wisely. In fact, this will be a business marriage. By the way, did the doctor mention you must pay for this relationship?

Quality System

Once the notified body has been selected, the device manufacturer must apply to the notified body for the quality management system (QMS) assessment. A few key components of the application process are:

1. The application must contain the manufacturer's name and address – duh;

2. Relevant product information must be provided;

3. A written declaration stating that multiple applications have not been filed with other notified bodies (only one application is permitted for each device marketed within the EU);

4. QMS documentation;

5. Ongoing QMS maintenance;

6. Technical documentation associated with EC type-examination certificates; and

7. A system for executing post-market surveillance activities.

Additionally, the QMS must be capable of supporting manufacturing operations that result in products meeting their essential requirements, and the Directive, as depicted within the EC type-examination certificate. Some of the documentation that needs to be considered for inclusion into the overall approach to QMS management are; the quality policy statement, the quality manual, procedures, work instructions, quality programs, plans, and records. In turn, the documentation created must be capable of supporting the device manufacturer as a whole. Even though Annex V formally delineates the requirements under the title "quality system," it is in reality a business management system. Not only should the QMS and the influence of a well-designed QMS has on manufacturing be considered, the positive influence a QMS exudes on the entire organization should be the fundamental goal.

Furthermore, the QMS and the associated documentation, as a minimum, must adequately describe and include:

1. The quality objectives;

2. Organizational structure;

3. Responsibilities and powers of management specific to product quality;

4. Testing being performed;

5. Traceability back to and calibration of test equipment;

6. Methods employed for monitoring the quality system;

7. Quality records and their fundamental management and retention;

8. The qualifications of all personnel;

9. Details associated with the final inspection, testing and acceptance of products; and

10. The monitoring and specific requirements for third-parties employed for final inspection and testing of products.

Finally, it is up to the notified body to assess the device manufacturer's QMS and ascertain if the system meets the requirements of the Directive. Remember, the goal is to have a fully implemented and approved QMS in accordance with ISO 13485:2003, elements of the MDD, and relevant harmonized standards, as applicable. The notified body is required to perform the assessment at the device manufacturer's facility "duh," with an assessment team that is trained and qualified. Upon completion of the assessment, the notified body will provide a written report containing observations, deviations, and conclusions. Deviations should be assigned, if warranted, prior to the departure of the assessment team. Once the QMS has been approved and certified by the notified body, it is the responsibility of the device manufacturer to inform the notified body of all changes made to the QMS. In fact, during each annual assessment one of the first questions the notified body will ask relates to changes made to the QMS since their previous visit. Hopefully, the answer is none, because notified bodies do not like surprises. By the way, did Dr. D mention notified bodies are paid by the device manufacturers to perform these assessments?

Surveillance

As Dr. D continues to age gracefully, so does my memory, or at least that is what the doctor would have the readers believe. In testing the doctor's memory, a few chapters ago, Dr. D mentioned that once a device manufacturer receives their certificate, reflecting a qualified QMS, the notified body does not just go away. As with other Annexes associated with the Directive, notified bodies are required to carry out inspections, as necessary, to ensure device manufacturers and their products remain in compliance with the Directive. Usually, the notified bodies plan these visits well in advance and provide an agenda for their visits (assessments). However, the notified bodies, under the Directive, have the authority to show up on a device manufacturer's door step –

unannounced. By the way, did Dr. D mention device manufacturers must pay their notified bodies for these visits?

Administrative Provisions

Similar to previously discussed Annexes, manufacturers or their Authorized European Representative must retain and make available certificates and documentation for a period of 5-years or 15-years (for implantable devices), after the last device has been manufactured. As a minimum, the following pieces of data must be retained: (a) declarations of conformity; (b) documentation defining the QMS or changes made to the QMS; (c) technical documentation (e.g., technical file); (d) reports and associated correspondences received from the notified body; and (e) EC type-examination certificates.

Applicability

In testing the doctor's memory again, the previous chapter contained a pointer to the inclusion and applicable of Class IIa devices as a salient element of Annex IV. Guess what? The same applicability clause for Class IIa devices is also a fundamental requirement for Annex V. During each of the friendly visits made to a device manufacturer's facility, by their notified body, technical files will be reviewed as part of the assessment. Notified bodies are required, in accordance with the Directive, to pull a sample of technical files, from each product family to review. That is why it is so darned important to keep technical files up-to-date. If a device manufacturer is blowing the proverbial dust off the cover before their notified body's assessment, they can expect to receive deviations as a result of the assessment. In fact, device manufacturers risk earning a major deviation as a result of the effort or should the doctor say, a lack of effort in maintaining technical files.

Human-Blood Derivatives

Not wanting to continue to sound like a broken record but obliged to do so because of the redundancy associated with several of the Annexes, products containing human-blood derivatives require additional testing. This testing must be performed at a State laboratory or an approved laboratory identified by a Member State. When in doubt, contact your notified body when testing is required. Hopefully, they will not charge you for just asking a question; but hey, these are challenging economic times.

What You Need to Do

For this chapter, doctor D will keep it simple, promise. Annex V, similar to all of the requirements delineated within the Directive, establishes basic expectations for device manufacturers and the responsibilities of notified bodies. That being said, the to do's are really simple and self-explanatory.

1. Do establish a compliant QMS.

2. Do ensure the QMS is assessed and hopefully, approved by a notified body.

3. Do ensure the CJO signs the Declaration of Conformity.

4. Do ensure the finished medical device packaging contains a CE Mark.

5. Do ensure a post-market surveillance system is established.

6. Do ensure adverse events are reported to the Competent Authorities (a.k.a., Vigilance Reports).

7. Do remember notified bodies are required to perform annual assessments.

8. Do remember that notified bodies can appear on a device manufacturer's door step unannounced.

9. Do remember to keep technical files current.

10. Do remember there is a mandated data retention requirement.

11. Do acknowledge the applicability component for Class IIa devices.

12. Do remember to employ approved laboratories for testing of products that contain human-blood derivatives.

Takeaways

I am sure by now; the readers are growing tired of the doctor's takeaways premised on common sense and regulations. In reality, there is just one takeaway and one takeaway only. Medical device manufacturers must design, develop, manufacturer, inspect, test, inspect some more, label, package, affix a CE Mark, ship, and distribute **"medical devices that are safe and effective - period!"** Obviously, quality systems and compliance to all applicable regulations are fundamental requirements. However, if a device manufacturer cannot **"make medical devices that are safe and effective,"** well what's the point?

"Having an approved QMS is a fundamental requirement for entrance into the European device market."

Chapter 33 – *Annex VI "EC Declaration of Conformity – Product Quality Assurance"*

Chapter Thirty-three – Annex VI

Annex V1 (*EC Declaration of Conformity – Product Quality Assurance*) of Council

Directive 93/42/EEC, a.k.a., the Medical Device Directive (MDD) delineates the

requirements for the performance of the quality system and specifically final inspection

and testing of product. As I am sure the readers are already finding out, there is

significant redundancy built into the Directive and the Annexes. Dr. D is also sure that

readers understand the application of the Annexes and their applicability for Class IIa,

Class IIb, and Class III products; and the importance of making the correct reference to

applicable Annexes in the signed EC Declaration of Conformity. Additionally, the doctor

hopes that by now readers understand the significance of ensuring medical devices meet

their essential requirements prior to having the Chief Jailable Officer (CJO) affixing his

or her signature to the declaration. Furthermore, Dr. D hopes that by now the readers

understand the duties and responsibilities of the notified bodies and Competent

Authorities, as prescribed within the Directive. Finally, the doctor hopes that by now the

readers understand the importance of affixing the CE mark onto approved products and

the ramifications of wrongly affixing CE marks to products. If the readers understand the

salient points the doctor has just made, then digesting all of the requirements nestled

within the Articles and Annexes should be an easy task, regardless of the perceived

redundancies. Although Dr. D does not consider himself to be overly prophetic, I can

offer multiple vaticinations (look-it-up) when device manufacturers fail to comply with

the MDD. Can you say market withdraw a.k.a., "RECALL" – Dr. D's favorite 6-letter

word? Can you say the revenue stream has just been interrupted? That being said, the

doctor promises not to bore the readers with guidance that is redundant from the previous chapters. Instead, Dr. D will climb onto his soap box and dance (just kidding). One of the neighborhood kids actually stole my soap box and used the wood for skateboards, so I will just write and be brief.

The MDD – 93/42/EEC

ANNEX VI – EC Declaration of Conformity – Product Quality Assurance

1. The manufacturer must ensure application of the quality system approved for the final inspection and testing of the product, as specified in Section 3 and must be subject to the surveillance referred to in Section 4. In addition, for products placed on the market in sterile condition, and only for those aspects of the manufacturing process designed to secure and maintain sterility, the manufacturer must apply the provisions of Annex V, Sections3 and 4.

2. The EC declaration of conformity is the part of the procedure whereby the manufacturer who fulfills the obligations imposed by Section 1 ensures and declares that the products concerned conform to the type described in the EC type-examination certificate and meet the provisions of this Directive which apply to them.

The manufacturer affixes the CE marking in accordance with Article 17 and draws up a written declaration of conformity. This declaration must cover one or more medical devices manufactured, clearly identified by means of product name, product code or other unambiguous reference, and be kept by the manufacturer. The CE marking must be accompanied by the identification number of the notified body which performs the tasks referred to in this Annex.

3. Quality system

3.1. The manufacturer lodges an application for assessment of his quality system with a notified body.

The application must include:

— *the name and address of the manufacturer,*

— *all the relevant information on the product or product category covered by the procedure,*

— *a written declaration specifying that no application has been lodged with any other notified body for the same products,*

— *the documentation on the quality system,*

— *an undertaking by the manufacturer to fulfill the obligations imposed by the quality system approved,*

— *an undertaking by the manufacturer to keep the approved quality system adequate and efficacious,*

— *where appropriate, the technical documentation on the types approved and a copy of the EC type-examination certificates,*

— *an undertaking by the manufacturer to institute and keep up to date a systematic procedure to review experience gained from devices in the post-production phase, including the provisions referred to in Annex X, and to implement appropriate means to apply any necessary corrective action. This undertaking must include an obligation for the manufacturer to notify the competent authorities of the following incidents immediately on learning of them:*

(i) any malfunction or deterioration in the characteristics and/or performance of a device, as well as any inadequacy in the labeling or the instructions for use which might lead to or might have led to the death of a patient or user or to a serious deterioration in his state of health;

(ii) any technical or medical reason connected with the characteristics or the performance of a device for the reasons referred to in subparagraph (i) leading to a systematic recall of devices of the same type by the manufacturer.

3.2. Under the quality system, each product or a representative sample of each batch is examined and the appropriate tests defined in the relevant standard(s) referred to in Article 5 or equivalent tests are carried out to ensure that the products conform to the type described in the EC type-examination certificate and fulfill the provisions of this Directive which apply to them. All the elements, requirements and provisions adopted by the manufacturer must be documented in a systematic and orderly manner in the form of written measures, procedures and instructions. This quality system documentation must permit uniform interpretation of the quality programs, quality plans, quality manuals and quality records.

It must include in particular an adequate description of:

— *the quality objectives and the organizational structure, responsibilities and powers of the managerial staff with regard to product quality,*

— *the examinations and tests that will be carried out after manufacture; it must be possible to trace back the calibration of the test equipment adequately,*

— *the methods of monitoring the efficient operation of the quality system,*

— *the quality records, such as reports concerning inspections, tests, calibration and the qualifications of the staff concerned, etc.,*

— *where the final inspection and testing of the products, or elements thereof, are carried out by a third party, the methods of monitoring the efficient operation of the quality system and in particular the type and extent of control applied to the third party.*

The aforementioned checks do not apply to those aspects of the manufacturing process designed to secure sterility.

3.3. The notified body audits the quality system to determine whether it meets the requirements referred to in section 3.2. It must presume that quality systems which implement the relevant harmonized standards conform to these requirements.

The assessment team must include at least one member with past experience of assessments of the technology concerned. The assessment procedure must include an inspection on the manufacturer's premises and, in duly substantiated cases, on the premises of the manufacturer's suppliers to inspect the manufacturing processes.

The decision must be notified to the manufacturer. It must contain the conclusions of the inspection and a reasoned assessment.

3.4. The manufacturer must inform the notified body which approved the quality system of any plan for substantial changes to the quality system.

The notified body must assess the changes proposed and verify whether after these changes the quality system will still meet the requirements referred to in Section 3.2.

After receiving the abovementioned information it must notify the manufacturer of its decision. This decision must contain the conclusions of the inspection and a reasoned assessment.

4. *Surveillance*

4.1. The aim of surveillance is to ensure that the manufacturer duly fulfills the obligations imposed by the approved quality system.

4.2. The manufacturer must allow the notified body access for inspection purposes to the inspection, testing and storage locations and supply it with all relevant information, in particular:

— the documentation on the quality system,

— the technical documentation,

— the quality records, such as inspection reports, test data, calibration data, qualification reports of the staff concerned, etc.

4.3. The notified body must periodically carryout appropriate inspections and assessments to make sure that the manufacturer applies the quality system and must supply the manufacturer with an assessment report.

4.4. In addition, the notified body may pay unannounced visits to the manufacturer. At the time of such visits, the notified body may, where necessary, carryout or ask for tests in order to check that the quality system is working properly and that the production conforms to the requirements of the Directive which apply to it. To this end, an adequate sample of the final products, taken on site by the notified body, must be examined and the appropriate tests defined in the relevant standard(s) referred to in Article 5 or equivalent tests must be carried out. Where one or more of the samples fails to conform, the notified body must take the appropriate measures.

It must provide the manufacturer with an inspection report and, if a test has been carried out, with a test report.

5. *Administrative provisions*

5.1. The manufacturer or his authorized representative must, for a period ending at least five years, and in the case of implantable devices at least 15 years, after the last product has been manufactured, make available to the national authorities:

— *the declaration of conformity,*

— *the documentation referred to in the seventh indent of Section 3.1,*

— *the changes referred to in Section 3.4,*

— *the decisions and reports from the notified body as referred to in the final indent of Section 3.4 and in Sections 4.3 and 4.4,*

— *where appropriate, the certificate of conformity referred to in Annex III.*

6. *Application to devices in Class IIa In line with Article 11(2), this Annex may apply to products in Class IIa, subject to the following:*

6.1. By way of derogation from Sections 2, 3.1 and 3.2, by virtue of the declaration of conformity the manufacturer ensures and declares that the products in Class IIa are manufactured inconformity with the technical documentation referred to in Section 3 of Annex VII and meet the requirements of this Directive which apply to them.

6.2. For devices in Class IIa the notified body shall assess, as part of the assessment in Section 3.3, the technical documentation as described in Section 3 of Annex VII for at least one representative sample for each device subcategory for compliance with the provisions of this Directive.

6.3. In choosing representative sample(s) the notified body shall take into account the novelty of the technology, similarities in design, technology, manufacturing and sterilization methods, the intended use and the results of any previous relevant assessments (e.g. with regard to physical, chemical or biological properties) that have been carried out in accordance with this Directive. The notified body shall document and keep available to the competent authority its rationale for the sample(s) taken.

6.4. Further samples shall be assessed by the notified body as part of the surveillance assessment referred to in Section 4.3.

What You Need to Know

Dr. D realizes the broken-record approach to teaching and providing guidance for regulations can be extremely boring. However, there is some value in the repetitive approach to learning. In the Marine Corps, we called the repetitive approach "learning through pain." In the medical device industry, the same approach can be called proactive learning. Regardless, the bulleted points depicted in this section capture what device manufacturers need to know and understand in regards to Annex VI; and yes – some of these points are redundant.

1. Device manufactures must establish an approved Quality Management System (QMS) to support the final inspection and testing of product.

2. A signed Declaration of Conformity is a salient requirement of Annex VI.

3. A CE Marking of conformity, containing the registration number of the device manufacturer's notified body, is a salient requirement of Annex VI.

4. The notified body is required to review and approve the device manufacturer's QMS.

5. The device manufacturer is required to monitor and maintain an effective QMS.

6. Device manufacturers are required to institute a post-market surveillance program.

7. Device manufacturers are required to notify the Competent Authorities when adverse events occur (vigilance reporting).

8. Device manufacturers are required to maintain quality records.

9. Notified bodies are required to perform surveillance audits after initial approval of a device manufacturer's QMS.

10. Device manufacturers are required to keep records specific to the Directive and certifications for a period of five years or 15-years (implantable devices).

What You Need to Do

First and foremost, device manufacturers need to develop and implement a world-class QMS that is fully compliant with ISO 13485:2003. Establishing an effective

QMS, regardless of the cost, should be considered the basic price of admission into the European device market.

Second, really put some significant effort into finding a competent notified body that your organization can work with effectively. I know Dr. D has made ongoing jokes about paying the notified bodies; however, they do work for the device manufacturer.

Third, when tossing an M61 fragmentation grenade, accuracy is not a factor providing the grenade is thrown in the direction of the bad guys. In medical devices, accuracy always counts, especially with the information placed in the declarations and certificates. Device manufacturers must ensure the declaration is complete and accurate prior to having the CJO affix his or her signature to the document.

Fourth, placing a CE mark on the product is extremely important. Make sure all of the applicable approvals and certifications have been received prior to affixing CE marks to the outer-most packaging of the finished medical device. If a device manufacturer has multiple notified bodies, please ensure the right CE mark is placed onto the correct product. Sounds like a pretty simple concept, right? The doctor has seen device manufacturers' royally screw up the placement of the CE mark by putting the wrong mark on the wrong product. Can you say "RECALL?"

Fifth, device manufacturers need to ensure technical files, and design dossiers are maintained to current standards; and the QMS monitored for ongoing effectiveness. Why? Because, as a minimum, the notified bodies are required to perform annual assessment visits. They also retain the authority to show up unannounced. Remember, device manufacturers are paying the notified bodies for this oversight.

Finally, record retention should always be considered a mission-critical requirement. Granted, the five and 15-year requirement delineated within the Directive is a given; however, all of the other records count too. Device manufacturers should establish an effective record retention procedure that delineates: (a) types of records; (b) record storage; (c) record retention duration; (d) protection from deterioration; and (e) audit requirements if records are stored at a third-party storage facility; e.g. Iron Mountain.

Takeaways

For device manufacturers, it all starts with the QMS. For device manufacturers, it all starts with the QMS. For device manufacturers, it all starts with the QMS. The repetitive learning process - got it? From Dr. D's perspective, the QMS should be premised on ISO 13485:2003. Regardless of the functional area; design, test, manufacturing, inspection, packaging, labeling, distribution, post-market surveillance, etc., it all starts with the QMS. All aspects of a device manufacturer's business must be controlled by established procedures. If the QMS is well-defined and employees are trained and performing tasks in accordance with documented procedures, then meeting the regulatory requirements of Annex VI and the Directive, as a whole, should be the proverbial "cake walk."

"Establishing an effective QMS, regardless of the cost, should be considered the basic price of admission into the European device market."

Chapter 34 – *Annex VII "EC Declaration of Conformity"*

Chapter Thirty-four – Annex VII

Annex VII (*EC Declaration of Conformity*) of Council Directive 93/42/EEC, a.k.a., the Medical Device Directive (MDD) is all about the Declaration of Conformity. Surprised? If you have managed to make it this far into my book, Dr. D is pretty sure you have comprehended the significance the MDD places on that tiny piece of paper called the EC Declaration of Conformity (DoC). I guess killing trees in pursuit of compliance is acceptable; although I am sure the ISO 14001 pundits might hold different beliefs. For those readers not having a chance to read the previous six chapters pertaining to the MDD Annexes; now would be a good time to catch up. So doctor, tell me why the DoC is so darned important? Not wanting to state the obvious, but obliged to do so, the DoC is a requirement mandated by the MDD and not an optional "nice-to-have." The information contained within the DoC is very specific in regards to device classification, applicable Annexes, part numbers, date approved, first lot shipped etc. Remember, the notified bodies employ this documentation, in part, to keep track of devices they have approved for entry into the EU. The notified bodies will not give permission to affix their CE marking of conformity until the technical file or design dossier has been reviewed, approved, and a declaration signed by the Chief Jailable Office (CJO) received. Additionally, if a device firm is racking up the vigilance reports in the EU, the notified body has the right to withdraw the certificate issued and force device manufacturers to remove the CE Mark from their products. Furthermore, the failure of a device manufacturer to maintain their quality management system (QMS) in compliance with ISO 13485:2003 can result in major deviations being issued by a notified body. These majors can also result in product being forced from the European Device market. Can you say RECALL? The best advice Dr. D can offer to save device manufacturers from

receiving objurgations (look-it-up) from the Competent Authorities is to fully comply

with all aspects of the Directive.

The MDD – 93/42/EEC

ANNEX VII – EC Declaration of Conformity

1. The EC declaration of conformity is the procedure whereby the manufacturer or his authorized representative who fulfills the obligations imposed by Section 2 and, in the case of products placed on the market in a sterile condition and devices with a measuring function, the obligations imposed by Section 5 ensures and declares that the products concerned meet the provisions of this Directive which apply to them.

2. The manufacturer must prepare the technical documentation described in Section3. The manufacturer or his authorized representative must make this documentation, including the declaration of conformity, available to the national authorities for inspection purposes for a period ending at least five years after the last product has been manufactured. In the case of implantable devices the period shall be at least 15 years after the last product has been manufactured.

3. The technical documentation must allow assessment of the conformity of the product with the requirements of the Directive. It must include in particular:

— *a general description of the product, including any variants planned and its intended use(s),*

— *design drawings, methods of manufacture envisaged and diagrams of components, sub-assemblies, circuits, etc.,*

— *the descriptions and explanations necessary to understand the above- mentioned drawings and diagrams and the operations of the product,*

— *the results of the risk analysis and a list of the standards referred to in Article5, applied in full or in part, and descriptions of the solutions adopted to meet the essential requirements of the Directive if the standards referred to in Article 5 have not been applied in full,*

— *in the case of products placed on the market in a sterile condition, description of the methods used and the validation report,*

— *the results of the design calculations and of the inspections carried out, etc.; if the device is to be connected to other device(s) in order to operate as intended, proof must be provided that it conforms to the essential requirements when connected to any such device(s) having the characteristics specified by the manufacturer,*

— *the solutions adopted as referred to in Annex I, Chapter I, Section 2,*

— *the pre-clinical evaluation,*

— *the clinical evaluation in accordance with Annex X,*

— *the label and instructions for use.*

4. The manufacturer shall institute and keep up to date a systematic procedure to review experience gained from devices in the post-production phase, including the provisions referred to in Annex X, and to implement appropriate means to apply any necessary corrective actions, taking account of the nature and risks in relation to the product. He shall notify the competent authorities of the following incidents immediately on learning of them:

(i) any malfunction or deterioration in the characteristics and/or performance of a device, as well as any inadequacy in the labeling or the instructions for use which might lead to or might have led to the death of a patient or user or to a serious deterioration in his state of health;

(ii) any technical or medical reason connected with the characteristics on the performance of a device for the reasons referred to in subparagraph (i) leading to systematic recall of devices of the same type by the manufacturer.

5. With products placed on the market in sterile condition and Class I devices with a measuring function, the manufacturer must observe not only the provisions laid down in this Annex but also one of the procedures referred to in Annex II, IV, V or VI. Application of the above- mentioned Annexes and the intervention by the notified body is limited to:

— *In the case of products placed on the market in sterile condition, only the aspects of manufacture concerned with securing and maintaining sterile conditions,*

— *In the case of devices with a measuring function, only the aspects of manufacture concerned with the conformity of the products with the metrological requirements.*

Section 6.1 of this Annex is applicable.

*6. **Application to devices in Class IIa** In line with Article 11 (2), this Annex may apply to products in Class IIa, subject to the following derogation: 6.1 where this Annex is applied in conjunction with the procedure referred to in Annex IV, V or VI, the declaration of conformity referred to in the abovementioned Annexes forms a single declaration. As regards the declaration based on this Annex, the manufacturer must ensure and declare that the product design meets the provisions of this Directive which apply to it.*

What You Need to Know

As Dr. D stated in the introduction for this chapter, Annex VII is all about the

paper, the DoC and supporting documentation. Gosh, the doctor hates killing trees. Now I

know much of this information is once again going to sound repetitive as many clauses nestled within the Annexes are applicable for a wide array of products. Regardless, Dr. D

will try not to bore the readers too badly as I attempt to point out the salient elements

device manufacturers need to know and understand in regards to Annex VII.

1. Device manufacturers are required to create and sign a DoC that clearly delineates

   product information, device classification, compliance with the MDD, and

   applicable Annexes. Try not to kill too many trees.

2. Device manufacturers are required to assemble technical documentation

   (technical files and design dossiers); and submit the documentation to their

   notified bodies for review and approval.

3. Device manufacturers are required to keep technical documentation, including

   DoC's and other documentation relevant to the Directive for a period of either

   five years or 15-years (for implantable devices). If a device manufacturer's

   products are hurting people, they can take it to the proverbial bank, the Competent

   Authorities are going to want to dive into technical documentation.

4. Since the technical documentation is being used by the notified body to assess a

   product's compliance to the Directive and applicable harmonized standards (as

   depicted within the Essential Requirements Checklist, a.k.a., the ERC), certain

   pieces of information must be included in the submission. As a minimum:

   a. General description of product and the intended use;

   b. Design information, methods employed for manufacturing, drawing,

      specifications, and diagrams;

   c. Description of salient functional performance and operational parameters as

      they pertain to the device and items depicted within b;

d. The application of risk analysis;

e. A compiled list of applicable standards employed to test and evaluate the product against essential requirements, remember the ERC;

f. Method of sterilization and sterilization validation process employed for sterile medical devices;

g. Results of all inspection and testing;

h. Testing of the product with ancillary devices, as appropriate;

i. Pre-clinical evaluation data;

j. Clinical data; and

k. The label and Instructions for Use (IFU); must be considered and if applicable, incorporated into the technical documentation package.

Similar to the other Annexes, post-market surveillance is a mission-critical requirement. Device manufactures are required to pursue corrective action when issues arise with their finished medical devices. Device malfunctions, deterioration over time, or other factors that influence the continued safety and efficacy of product must be addressed. Devices causing death or serious injury to the patient or user must be reported to the Competent Authorities. Remember, the EU has been working on an improved system for collection and analyzing vigilance reports. This improved competency is forcing medical device manufacturers to expedite product corrections or quickly remove offending product from market.

Class I sterile devices and devices with a measuring function must comply with Annex VII and the provisions depicted within Annexes II, IV, V, or VI, as applicable. Finally, there is once again an applicability element for Class IIa product.

What You Need to Do

For those of you that had the pleasure of reading the previous chapter, the neighborhood kids felt pretty bad about stealing the old doctor's soapbox to build skateboard decks, so they decided to build me a new podium. That being said, Dr. D will climb onto his new podium and begin to pontificate. I only hope it holds the doctor's weight. The doctor loves his barbeque and Jack Daniel's. Anyhow, what Dr. D is about to write is not some well-kept state-secret. Well maybe it is, because the doctor continues to see device manufacturers struggle with compliance issues. The device market sandbox that a device manufacturer chooses to play in does not matter; however, compliance with the regulations applicable to that sandbox continues to be mandatory. Compliance with Annex VII of the MDD is no exception. That being said, a few of the "must dos" for device manufacturers are:

1. The CJO must complete and sign a DoC;

2. Technical documentation (technical file or design dossier) must be prepared and submitted to the notified body for review and approval;

3. Technical documentation must be retained in accordance with the prescribed time, five or fifteen years;

4. Pre-clinical and clinical evaluations, premised on well-written protocols and evaluated with recognized statistical methodologies, are required as applicable;

5. Class I devices with a measuring function count, as do sterile devices so make sure they are tested in accordance with the appropriate Annexes; and

6. Once again, do not forget about the applicability clause for Class IIa devices.

If a device manufacturer does not have the resources or is not willing to invest in executing the appropriate testing, inspection, verification, validation, creation of reports and technical documentation, then just maybe the device arena is the wrong venue. Dr. D would recommend horseshoes, but I am absolutely sure, they have strict standards too!

Takeaways

First off readers be patient, there are just five more chapters remaining in this book, with the last pertaining to CE Mark construction, fun-fun. As Dr. D leaps off his newly constructed podium (thank you skate boarders), the message of compliance remains consistent and will never change. The goal of any device regulation and regulatory body, regardless of the country of origin; is the protection of public health by ensuring medical devices are safe and effective. It does not matter if it is a splinter needing to be pulled from the tongue of a patient with strep throat due to a faulty tongue depressor, or an angioplasty balloon catheter that fails to inflate in the hands of a skilled cardiologist. In each case, a device has failed to perform in its intended use. On a serious note, and Dr. D can be serious on occasion, I have always approached the industry from the perspective of would I be comfortable having a family member or close friend on the receiving end of a medical device that I directly influenced the quality or reliability. If Dr. D cannot wake up, look in the mirror, and state an unequivocal "**Yes**" then I am in the wrong business.

"The goal of any device regulation and regulatory body, regardless of the country of origin; is the protection of public health by ensuring medical devices are safe and effective."

Chapter 35 – *Annex VIII*

"Statement Concerning Devices for Special Purposes"

Chapter Thirty-five – Annex VIII

Annex VIII (Statement Concerning Devices for Special Purposes) of Council Directive 93/42/EEC, a.k.a., the Medical Device Directive (MDD) delineates the requirements for custom-made devices and/or investigational devices intended specifically for employment in clinical investigations. Similar to the Investigational Device Exemption (IDE) category used for devices intended for a clinical trial application in the United States, the MDD has specific requirements to ensure product safety and efficacy is sustained for similar devices used within the European Union (EU). If you have made it this far through the book then you are used to Dr. D's occasional sprinkling of homiletic aphorisms (look-it-up) throughout each of the chapters. This chapter will be no different. Remember, "Hindsight is always 20/20."

The MDD – 93/42/EEC

ANNEX VIII – Statement Concerning Devices for Special Purposes

1. For custom-made devices or for devices intended for clinical investigations the manufacturer or his authorized representative must draw up the statement containing the information stipulated in Section 2.

2. The statement must contain the following information:

2.1. for custom-made devices:

— *the name and address of the manufacturer,*

— *data allowing identification of the device in question,*

— *a statement that the device is intended for exclusive use by a particular patient, together with the name of the patient,*

— *the name of the medical practitioner or other authorized person who made out the prescription and, where applicable, the name of the clinic concerned,*

— *the specific characteristics of the product as indicated by the prescription,*

— *a statement that the device in question conforms to the essential requirements set out in Annex I and, where applicable, indicating which essential requirements have not been fully met, together with the grounds;*

2.2. for devices intended for the clinical investigations covered by Annex X:

— *data allowing identification of the device in question,*

— *the clinical investigation plan,*

— *the investigator's brochure,*

— *the confirmation of insurance of subjects,*

— *the documents used to obtain informed consent,*

— *a statement indicating whether or not the device incorporates, as an integral part, a substance or human blood derivative referred to in Section 7.4 of Annex I,*

— *a statement indicating whether or not the device is manufactured utilizing tissues of animal origin as referred to in Directive 2003/32/EC,*

— *the opinion of the ethics committee concerned and details of the aspects covered by its opinion,*

— *the name of the medical practitioner or other authorized person and of the institution responsible for the investigations,*

— *the place, starting date and scheduled duration for the investigations,*

— *a statement that the device in question conforms to the essential requirements apart from the aspects covered by the investigations and that, with regard to these aspects, every precaution has been taken to protect the health and safety of the patient.*

3. The manufacturer must also undertake to keep available for the competent national authorities:

3.1. For custom-made devices, documentation, indicating manufacturing site(s) and allowing an understanding of the design, manufacture and performances of the product, including the expected performances, so as to allow assessment of conformity with the requirements of this Directive.

The manufacturer must take all the measures necessary to ensure that the manufacturing process produces products which are manufactured in accordance with the documentation mentioned in the first paragraph;

3.2. For devices intended for clinical investigations, the documentation must contain:

— *a general description of the product and its intended use,*

— *design drawings, methods of manufacture envisaged, in particular as regards sterilization, and diagrams of components, sub-assemblies, circuits, etc.,*

— *the descriptions and explanations necessary to understand the above-mentioned drawings and diagrams and the operation of the product,*

— *the results of the risk analysis and a list of the standards referred to in Article5, applied in full or in part, and descriptions of the solutions adopted to meet the essential requirements of this Directive if the standards referred to in Article 5 have not been applied,*

— *if the device incorporates, as an integral part, a substance or human blood derivative referred to in Section 7.4 of Annex I, the data on the tests conducted in this connection which are required to assess the safety, quality and usefulness of that substance or human blood derivative, taking account of the intended purpose of the device,*

— *if the device is manufactured utilizing tissues of animal origin as referred to in Directive 2003/32/EC, the risk management measures in this connection which have been applied to reduce the risk of infection,*

— *the results of the design calculations, and of the inspections and technical tests carried out, etc.*

The manufacturer must take all the measures necessary to ensure that the manufacturing process produces products which are manufactured in accordance with the documentation referred to in the first paragraph of this Section.

The manufacturer must authorize the assessment, or audit where necessary, of the effectiveness of these measures.

4. The information contained in the declarations concerned by this Annex shall be kept for a period of time of at least five years. In the case of implantable devices the period shall be at least 15 years.

5. For custom-made devices, the manufacturer must undertake to review and document experience gained in the post-production phase, including the provisions referred to in Annex X, and to implement appropriate means to apply any necessary corrective action. This undertaking must include an obligation for the manufacturer to notify the competent authorities of the following incidents immediately on learning of them and the relevant corrective actions:

(i) any malfunction or deterioration in the characteristics and/or performance of a device, as well as any inadequacy in the labeling or the instructions for use which might lead to or might have led to the death of a patient or user or to a serious deterioration in his state of health;

(ii) any technical or medical reason connected with the characteristics or performance of a device for the reasons referred to in subparagraph (i) leading to systematic recall of devices of the same type by the manufacturer.

What You Need to Know

No surprises here, but device manufacturers need to work through their notified bodies to ensure the basic requirements associated with Annex VIII are achieved prior to shipment into the EU. For custom-made devices and investigational devices, the process commences with the generation of a statement of conformance that contains product-specific information. For custom-made devices, this statement must contain:

1. The name and address of the actual manufacturer;

2. Data that can be employed to quickly identify the custom-made device;

3. A written statement that clearly defines that the custom device is intended for use on a specific patient, including the patient's name;

4. The name of the clinician prescribing the device and the address of the healthcare facility where the procedure will take place;

5. The operating / performance characteristics of the custom-made device, as delineated by the prescription; and

6. A statement that delineates the custom-made device meets essential requirements, as applicable.

For devices intended to be used in clinical investigations (trials), written statements, from the device manufacturer, are also required prior to these devices being given access to the EU. As a minimum, data needing to support the approval of devices intended for clinical use are:

1. Data that can be employed to quickly identify the investigational device;

2. The protocol to be employed in the clinical trial;

3. Insurance confirmation for clinical trial participants;

4. Informed consent documentation;

5. Statements acknowledging the use of human-blood derivatives or tissue of animal origin within the investigational device, if applicable;

6. Opinion of the ethics committee (from the applicable institution) pertaining to the actual protocol; and

7. The actual name of the practitioner responsible for clinical trial oversight, execution, the address of the clinical trial location, starting date, and expected duration of the clinical trial; and

8. A statement to the fact that the clinical device meets essential requirements and the device is safe and effective for its intended use.

Data and Documentation Requirements

For custom-made devices and investigational devices, there is also a requirement for specific pieces of data to be retained, just in case the Competent Authorities want to take a look. For custom-made devices, examples of data and documentation requiring to be retained are:

1. Manufacturing location(s);

2. Design documentation;

3. Manufacturing documentation e.g., manufacturing processes;

4. Inspection and testing methodologies applied to ascertain custom-made device performances; and

5. Any and all documentation that supports claims of conformance to the Directive.

For investigational devices, additional data requirements are mandated by the Directive. In fact, these additional requirements mimic those of a technical file and/or design dossier. Since a positive outcome is always the hope of any clinical trial, Dr. D recommends just biting the bullet and doing the right thing from the start; and commence with the assembly of the technical file and/or dossier at inception. If this approach is followed, then upon conclusion of the trial, only the clinical data will need to be added. That being said, as a minimum, the documentation needed to support the investigation device are:

1. The description of the medical device, including the intended use of the device;

2. Design drawings (including design calculations), manufacturing processes, sterilization, critical components, subassemblies, inspection activities, and testing;

3. Application of risk analysis (make sure to employ ISO 14971:2009);

4. A compiled list of applicable standards, e.g., essential requirements checklist;

5. Additional testing performed, if the device contains a human blood derivative; and

6. Identification and risk assessment of animal tissue, if employed as part of the investigational device.

Remember, just because devices covered under Annex VIII have been given special names, their own Annex, and some dispensation in regards to regulatory requirements, the expectation is that the same inherent controls applied as part of routine manufacturing of approved medical devices are applicable to these devices. This includes audits to ensure the overall effectiveness of the tools employed in the design, manufacture, inspection, and testing of investigational devices.

Identical to the other Annexes, there is a data retention requirement for data used to support declarations. For most devices the standard requirement is five years. For implantable devices, the retention period is 15-years. Finally, and identical to previous Annexes, there is a post-market surveillance requirement. Manufacturers are expected to pursue appropriate corrective action when: (a) device malfunctions occur; (b) device performance characteristics have deteriorated; and (c) device performance has resulted in serious injury or death of the patient or user. Remember, these adverse events must be reported in accordance with the European Vigilance Reporting process. Failure to report will surely agitate the Competent Authorities. Devices that fail to meet expected safety and efficacy requirements should be withdrawn, a.k.a., RECALLED!

What You Need to Do

Once again, Dr. D will share a not so well-kept secret. For medical device that are safe and effective, it is all about a robust design anchored in the application of adequate design verification and design validation methodologies. You can quote the doctor when I say; "A crappy design equates to a crappy device." As an old quality guy, Dr. D has experienced, first-hand, the results of custom-made and clinical devices, regardless of the robustness of the design, being built on prototype production lines with limited controls in place. For some reason device manufacturers often equate "prototype" to "no quality oversight required" Granted, this approach may be effective for building the initial path-finder units prior to design transfer. However, for building units that will be used on patients, quality oversight is required. This includes the use of calibrated instrumentation, trained operators, and manufacturing processes that have been appropriately validated. Why? Because under Annex VIII of the Directive, device manufacturers cannot build custom-made or investigational devices in the proverbial garage. Accuracy and documentation count!

One aspect of Dr. D's business is the performance of supplier audits and internal audits. I always cringe when I peek into the engineering lab or assess prototype manufacturing lines for the same reasons depicted in the previous paragraph. That being said, the doctor has a solution. Device manufacturers should have a dedicated pilot line for the manufacturing of custom-made and/or investigational devices. This line may not be operational 24/7; however, when needed, device manufacturers can quickly reassign assemblers, inspectors and technicians for brief periods of time to meet short-term demand. The pilot line should be considered a controlled line with all of the device manufacturer's assembly, inspection, testing, training, calibration, and validation procedures in full-force. All product manufactured on this pilot line should have the appropriate manufacturing travelers, inspection results, test results, and associated documentation that will form the foundation of the device History Record (DHR). One final note; do not forget about including the pilot line into the internal audit program.

Takeaways

As you can gather from Dr. D's section on "What You Need to Do," manufacturing special devices always strikes a chord with the doctor and sometimes the notes are sour. Just because Annex VIII delineates requirements for custom-made and investigational devices in a way that can be interpreted as manufacturing a device in a less than compliant environment, nothing could be further from the truth. Climbing back onto my pulpit to pontificate, Dr. D will once again emphatically state, "Medical device must be safe and effective in their intended use!" In reviewing Annex VIII, although the requirements have been tailored for custom-made and investigational devices, there is nothing nestled in the Annex that remotely indicates exceptions from the level of quality in the design, manufacturing, inspection, or testing of medical devices. That being said, the doctor will close out this chapter's guidance with just one takeaway. Custom-made and investigational devices are used to treat patients. They must be designed, manufactured, inspected, and tested in a manner that results in a device that is safe and effective. That means adequate controls must be in place.

"A crappy design equates to a crappy device."

Chapter 36 – *Annex IX*

"Classification Criteria"

Chapter Thirty-six – Annex IX

Annex IX (Classification Criteria) of Council Directive 93/42/EEC, a.k.a., the Medical

Device Directive (MDD) delineates: (a) detailed definitions for the classification rules;

(b) rule implementation; and (c) rule classifications; employed in support of the

Directive. In support of this chapter, Dr. D believes it would be absolutely insane to

provide detailed guidance on definitions and rules; and a waste of the doctor's

coruscating (look-it-up) prose. In fact, Dr. D would equate such an effort to someone

attempting to provide guidance on the definitions depicted in a Merriam-Webster's

Dictionary or equally futile attempts made to drain the Pacific Ocean. That being said,

Dr. D will acknowledge that the 18 rules associated with Annex IX are mandatory. Yes,

Dr. D understands that some folks just do not like to play by the rules. However, in the

medical-device sandbox, device manufacturers that fail to adhere to the rules will soon

shudder the windows and doors of their empty manufacturing facilities. In short, play by

the rules or go home.

The MDD – 93/42/EEC

ANNEX IX – Classification Criteria

I. DEFINITIONS

*1. **Definitions for the classification rules***

1.1. Duration

Transient

Normally intended for continuous use for less than 60 minutes.

Short term

Normally intended for continuous use for not more than 30 days.

Long term

Normally intended for continuous use for more than 30 days.

1.2. Invasive devices

Invasive device

A device which, in whole or in part, penetrates inside the body, either through a body orifice or through the surface of the body.

Body orifice

Any natural opening in the body, as well as the external surface of the eyeball, or any permanent artificial opening, such as a stoma.

Surgically invasive device

An invasive device which penetrates inside the body through the surface of the body, with the aid or in the context of a surgical operation.

For the purposes of this Directive devices other than those referred to in the previous subparagraph and which produce penetration other than through an established body orifice, shall be treated as surgically invasive devices.

Implantable device

Any device which is intended:

— to be totally introduced into the human body or,

— to replace an epithelial surface or the surface of the eye,

by surgical intervention which is intended to remain in place after the procedure.

Any device intended to be partially introduced into the human body through surgical intervention and intended to remain in place after the procedure for at least 30 days is also considered an implantable device.

1.3. Reusable surgical instrument

Instrument intended for surgical use by cutting, drilling, sawing, scratching, scraping, clamping, retracting, clipping or similar procedures, without connection to any active medical device and which can be reused after appropriate procedures have been carried out.

1.4. Active medical device

Any medical device operation of which depends on a source of electrical energy or any source of power other than that directly generated by the human body or gravity and which acts by converting this energy. Medical devices intended to transmit energy, substances or other elements between an active medical device and the patient, without any significant change, are not considered to be active medical devices. Standalone software is considered to be an active medical device.

1.5. Active therapeutical device

Any active medical device, whether used alone or in combination with other medical devices, to support, modify, replace or restore biological functions or structures with a view to treatment or alleviation of an illness, injury or handicap.

1.6. Active device for diagnosis

Any active medical device, whether used alone or in combination with other medical devices, to supply information for detecting, diagnosing, monitoring or treating physiological conditions, states of health, illnesses or congenital deformities.

1.7. Central circulatory system

For the purposes of this Directive, 'central circulatory system' means the following vessels:

arteriae pulmonales, aorta ascendens, arcus aorta, aorta descendens to the bifurcation aortae, arteriae coronariae, arteria carotis communis, arteria carotis externa, arteria carotis interna, arteriae cerebrales, truncus brachiocephalicus, venae cordis, venae pulmonales, vena cava superior, vena cava inferior.

1.8. Central nervous system

For the purposes of this Directive, 'central nervous system' means brain, meninges and spinal cord.

II. IMPLEMENTING RULES

2. Implementing rules

2.1. Application of the classification rules shall be governed by the intended purpose of the devices.

2.2. If the device is intended to be used in combination with another device, the classification rules shall apply separately to each of the devices. Accessories are classified in their own right separately from the device with which they are used.

2.3. Software, which drives a device or influences the use of a device, falls automatically in the same class.

2.4. If the device is not intended to be used solely or principally in a specific part of the body, it must be considered and classified on the basis of the most critical specified use.

2.5. If several rules apply to the same device, based on the performance specified for the device by the manufacturer, the strictest rules resulting in the higher classification shall apply.

2.6. In calculating the duration referred to in Section 1.1 of Chapter I, continuous use means 'an uninterrupted actual use of the device for the intended purpose'. However where usage of a device is discontinued in order for the device to be replaced immediately by the same or an identical device this shall be considered an extension of the continuous use of the device.

III. CLASSIFICATION

1. Non-invasive devices

1.1. Rule 1

All non-invasive devices are in Class I, unless one of the rules set out hereinafter applies.

1.2. Rule 2

All non-invasive devices intended for channeling or storing blood, body liquids or tissues, liquids or gases for the purpose of eventual infusion, administration or introduction into the body are in Class IIa:

— *if they may be connected to an active medical device in Class IIa or a higher class,*

    — *if they are intended for use for storing or channeling blood or other body liquids or for storing organs, parts of organs or body tissues, in all other cases they are in Class I.*

1.3. Rule 3

All non-invasive devices intended for modifying the biological or chemical composition of blood, other body liquids or other liquids intended for infusion into the body are in Class IIb, unless the treatment consists of filtration, centrifugation or exchanges of gas, heat, in which case they are in Class IIa.

1.4. Rule 4

All non-invasive devices which come into contact with injured skin:

— *are in Class I if they are intended to be used as a mechanical barrier, for compression or for absorption of exudates,*

— *are in Class IIb if they are intended to be used principally with wounds which have breached the dermis and can only heal by secondary intent,*

    — *are in Class IIa in all other cases, including devices principally intended to manage the micro-environment of a wound.*

2. Invasive devices

2.1. Rule 5

All invasive devices with respect to body orifices, other than surgically invasive devices and which are not intended for connection to an active medical device or which are intended for connection to an active medical device in Class I:

— are in Class I if they are intended for transient use,

— are in Class IIa if they are intended for short-term use, except if they are used in the oral cavity as far as the pharynx, in an ear canal up to the eardrum or in a nasal cavity, in which case they are in Class I,

— are in Class IIb if they are intended for long-term use, except if they are used in the oral cavity as far as the pharynx, in an ear canal up to the eardrum or in a nasal cavity and are not liable to be absorbed by the mucous membrane, in which case they are in Class IIa.

All invasive devices with respect to body orifices, other than surgically invasive devices, intended for connection to an active medical device in Class IIa or a higher class, are in Class IIa.

2.2. Rule 6

All surgically invasive devices intended for transient use are in Class IIa unless they are:

— intended specifically to control, diagnose, monitor or correct a defect of the heart or of the central circulatory system through direct contact with these parts of the body, in which case they are in Class III,

— reusable surgical instruments, in which case they are in Class I,

— intended specifically for use indirect contact with the central nervous system, in which case they are in Class III,

— intended to supply energy in the form of ionizing radiation in which case they are in Class IIb,

— intended to have a biological effector to be wholly or mainly absorbed in which case they are in Class IIb,

— intended to administer medicines by means of a delivery system, if this is done in a manner that is potentially hazardous taking account of the mode of application, in which case they are in Class IIb.

2.3. Rule 7

All surgically invasive devices intended for short-term use are in Class IIa unless they are intended:

— either specifically to control, diagnose, monitor or correct a defect of the heart or of the central circulatory system through direct contact with these parts of the body, in which case they are in Class III,

— or specifically for use indirect contact with the central nervous system, in which case they are in Class III,

— or to supply energy in the form of ionizing radiation in which case they are in Class IIb,

— or to have a biological effector to be wholly or mainly absorbed in which case
    they are in Class III,

— or to undergo chemical change in the body, except if the devices are placed in the teeth,
    or to administer medicines, in which case they are in Class IIb.

2.4. Rule 8

All implantable devices and long-term surgically invasive devices are in Class IIb
unless they are intended:

— to be placed in the teeth, in which case they are in Class IIa,

— to be used indirect contact with the heart, the central circulatory system or the
    central nervous system, in which case they are in Class III,

— to have a biological effector to be wholly or mainly absorbed, in which case
    they are in Class III,

— or to undergo chemical change in the body, except if the devices are placed in
    the teeth, or to administer medicines, in which case they are in Class III.

3. Additional rules applicable to active devices

3.1. Rule 9

All active therapeutic devices intended to administer or exchange energy are in   Class
IIa unless their characteristics are such that they may administer or   exchange energy to or
from the human body in a potentially hazardous way,   taking account of the nature, the
density and site of application of the energy, in   which case they are in Class IIb.

All active devices intended to control or monitor the performance of active
therapeutic devices in Class IIb, or intended directly to influence the performance
of such devices are in Class IIb.

3.2. Rule 10

Active devices intended for diagnosis are in Class IIa:

— if they are intended to supply energy which will be absorbed by the human
    body, except for devices used to illuminate the patient's body, in the visible
    spectrum,

— if they are intended to image in vivo distribution of radio pharmaceuticals,

— if they are intended to allow direct diagnosis or monitoring of vital
    physiological processes, unless they are specifically intended for monitoring of vital
    physiological parameters, where the nature of variations is such that it could result in
    immediate danger to the patient, for instance variations in cardiac performance,
    respiration, activity of CNS in which case they are in Class IIb.

Active devices intended to emit ionizing radiation and intended for diagnostic and therapeutic interventional radiology including devices which control or monitor such devices, or which directly influence their performance, are in Class IIb.

Rule 11

All active devices intended to administer and/or remove medicines, body liquids or other substances to or from the body are in Class IIa, unless this is done in a manner:

— that is potentially hazardous, taking account of the nature of the substances involved, of the part of the body concerned and of the mode of application in which case they are in Class IIb.

3.3. Rule 12

All other active devices are in Class I.

4. Special Rules

4.1. Rule 13

All devices incorporating, as an integral part, a substance which, if used separately, can be considered to be a medicinal product, as defined in Article 1 of Directive 2001/83/EC, and which is liable to act on the human body with action ancillary to that of the devices, are in Class III.

All devices incorporating, as an integral part, a human blood derivative are in   Class III.

4.2. Rule 14

All devices used for contraception or the prevention of the transmission of sexually transmitted diseases are in Class IIb, unless they are implantable or long term invasive devices, in which case they are in Class III.

4.3. Rule 15

All devices intended specifically to be used for disinfecting, cleaning, rinsing or, ` when appropriate, hydrating contact lenses are in Class IIb.

All devices intended specifically to be used for disinfecting medical devices are in Class IIa. Unless they are specifically to be used for disinfecting invasive devices in which case they are in Class IIb.

This rule does not apply to products that are intended to clean medical devices other than contact lenses by means of physical action.

4.4. Rule 16

Devices specifically intended for recording of X-ray diagnostic images are in Class IIa.

4.5. Rule 17

All devices manufactured utilizing animal tissues or derivatives rendered non-viable are Class III except where such devices are intended to come into contact with intact skin only.

5. Rule 18

By derogation from other rules, blood bags are in Class IIb.

What You Need to Know

Device manufacturers not familiar with entering product into the European device market need to understand and grasp the significance of the rules delineated under Article IX. Probably the most salient point Dr. D can make in regards to Annex IX is the linkage between rules and device classification. For example, Rule 1 - applicable for non-invasive devices is specific to all Class I devices, unless otherwise noted. Rule 3 is typically associated with Class IIb devices, unless a device is covered by another rule due to a specific intended use. Under Rule 8, if a device can be categorized as an implantable and as a long-term surgically invasive device; and the device comes into direct contact with the heart, then the device classification will be a Class III.

So why are the definitions, rules and classifications so darned important? Collectively, this information is used by the notified bodies as part of the review and certification process. Additionally, this information will be depicted within the manufacturer's Declaration of Conformity, signed by the Chief Jailable Officer (CJO), the notified body certification, and within the technical file or design dossier. Furthermore, under the changes to the Directive that went into effect in March of 2010, manufacturers of Class III and some Class IIa and IIb devices are going to be hard-pressed to receive device approval if a clinical trial has not been performed. Finally, driven by the rules and classification, device manufacturers are expected to assembly either the technical file (Class IIa and IIb) or design dossier (Class III). This technical documentation will be shipped off to their notified body for review and approval. In repeating a point that Dr. D has made on multiple occasions, long-gone are the days when medical device manufacturers could self-certify Class IIa and Class IIb products. In today's regulatory climate, notified bodies are reviewing technical files prior to the allowance of their CE mark of registration being affixed to medical devices. Under amendments made to the directive, notified bodies are now required to audit a statistically significant sample of technical files during their surveillance audits. By the way, did Dr. D fail to mention device manufacturers pay the notified bodies for these reviews and audits? Just kidding folks, I believe the doctor has risen to broken-record god status with comments relating to the payment of notified bodies for their services. However, you pay them and they work for you. Do not be afraid to remind them of the relationship occasionally, especially the payment part.

What You Need to Do

For starters, if a device manufacturer has not selected a notified body, Dr. D recommends picking a recognized organization with significant experience and familiarization with products similar to yours. Organizations such as TUV-R and BSI (the doctor is not a paid spokesperson for these organizations) are extremely competent and knowledgeable. The notified bodies can provide the necessary guidance to ensure manufacturers select the correct rules and classifications for their products. Ultimately, it will be these same notified bodies that review the technical documentation, approve the applications, and issue the certifications. Remember, medical devices cannot ship into the

EU without the CE mark affixed to the outermost packaging. Notified bodies will not allow the affixing of their CE mark of registration until all reviews have been completed, the declaration signed by the CJO received, and the certificates issued.

Takeaways

Dr. D had a chance to speak with a friend of his that works for a well-recognized notified body. Yes, Dr. D does have friends. One of the concerns he shared with me was the ongoing issues surrounding device manufacturer's declarations of conformity and the errors being made. That being said, the take away from this chapter pertains to the accuracy of the declaration. For starters, device manufacturers need to ensure all of the information depicted within the declaration is factual and accurate. This includes the topic of this chapter, rules and classifications. Since the CJO is affixing his or her John Hancock to the bottom of each declaration, it would behoove these individuals to ensure the information is correct. Dr. D has first-hand experience reviewing and rejecting literally hundreds of declarations due to errors, i.e., typos, wrong rule, wrong classification, wrong part number, missing first batch data, wrong notified body, etc. Frankly, the doctor found the number of errors to be embarrassing. Remember, accuracy counts, unless you are throwing a grenade then "close but no cigars" might be acceptable.

"You pay the Notified Bodies, they work for you. Do not be afraid to remind them of the relationship occasionally, especially the payment part."

Chapter 37 – *Annex X*

"Clinical Evaluation"

Chapter Thirty-seven – Annex X

Annex X (Clinical Evaluation) of Council Directive 93/42/EEC, a.k.a., the Medical

Device Directive (MDD) delineates the need to ascertain the safety and efficacy of a

medical device through the employment of clinical research and data. Depending on the

device classification and intended device use, the clinical evaluation can be premised on

the search and subsequent analysis of clinical data for similar or predicate devices. For

Class III devices or devices categorized as implantable, device manufacturers better break

out their check books and be prepared to support a complete clinical investigation (trial).

A few of the more perspicacious (look-it-up) device manufacturers will understand the

need for performing a clinical trial early in the planning process. Some device

manufacturers will fail to understand the Annex X requirements, delineated under the

Directive, and experience first-hand the joys of having an application to market a new

device, made to their notified body, rejected. Can you say, "No European market entry?"

Dr. D believes the chances are pretty good that no market will open their doors to a

device obviously needing a clinical investigation to support safety and efficacy; good

luck in trying.

The MDD – 93/42/EEC

ANNEX X – Clinical Evaluation

1. General provisions

1.1. As a general rule, confirmation of conformity with the requirements concerning the characteristics and performances referred to in Sections 1 and 3 of Annex I, under the normal conditions of use of the device, and the evaluation of the side-effects and of the acceptability of the benefit/risk ratio referred to in Section 6 of Annex I, must be based on clinical data. The evaluation of this data, hereinafter referred to as 'clinical evaluation', where appropriate taking account of any relevant harmonized standards, must follow a defined and methodologically sound procedure based on:

1.1.1. *Either a critical evaluation of the relevant scientific literature currently available relating to the safety, performance, design characteristics and intended purpose of the device, where:*

— *there is demonstration of equivalence of the device to the device to which the data relates, and*

— *the data adequately demonstrate compliance with the relevant essential requirements.*

1.1.2. *Or a critical evaluation of the results of all clinical investigations made.*

1.1.3. *Or a critical evaluation of the combined clinical data provided in 1.1.1 and1.1.2.*

1.1a *In the case of implantable devices and devices in Class III clinical investigations shall be performed unless it is duly justified to rely on existing clinical data.*

1.1b *The clinical evaluation and its outcome shall be documented. This documentation shall be included and/or fully referenced in the technical documentation of the device.*

1.1c *The clinical evaluation and its documentation must be actively updated with data obtained from the post-market surveillance. Where post-market clinical follow-up as part of the post-market surveillance plan for the device is not deemed necessary, this must be duly justified and documented.*

1.1d *Where demonstration of conformity with essential requirements based on clinical data is not deemed appropriate, adequate justification for any such exclusion has to be given based on risk management output and under consideration of the specifics of the device/body interaction, the clinical performances intended and the claims of the manufacturer. Adequacy of demonstration of conformity with the essential requirements by performance evaluation, bench testing and preclinical evaluation alone has to be duly substantiated.*

1.2. *All the data must remain confidential, in accordance with the provisions of Article 20.*

2. *Clinical investigations*

2.1. *Objectives The objectives of clinical investigation are:*

— *to verify that, under normal conditions of use, the performance of the devices conform to those referred to in Section 3 of Annex I, and*

— *to determine any undesirable side-effects, under normal conditions of use, and assess whether they constitute risks when weighed against the intended performance of the device.*

2.2. *Ethical considerations*

Clinical investigations must be carried out in accordance with the Helsinki Declaration adopted by the 18th World Medical Assembly in Helsinki, Finland, in 1964, as last amended by the World Medical Assembly. It is mandatory that all measures relating to the protection of human subjects are carried out in the spirit of the Helsinki Declaration. This includes every step in the clinical investigation from first consideration of the need and justification of the study to publication of the results.

2.3. Methods

2.3.1. Clinical investigations must be performed on the basis of an appropriate plan of investigation reflecting the latest scientific and technical knowledge and defined in such a way as to confirm or refute the manufacturer's claims for the device; these investigations must include an adequate number of observations to guarantee the scientific validity of the conclusions.

2.3.2. The procedures used to perform the investigations must be appropriate to the device under examination.

2.3.3. Clinical investigations must be performed in circumstances similar to the normal conditions of use of the device.

2.3.4. All the appropriate features, including those involving the safety and performances of the device, and its effect on patients must be examined.

2.3.5. All serious adverse events must be fully recorded and immediately notified to all competent authorities of the Member States in which the clinical investigation is being performed.

2.3.6. The investigations must be performed under the responsibility of a medical practitioner or another authorized qualified person in an appropriate environment. The medical practitioner or other authorized person must have access to the technical and clinical data regarding the device. 2.3.7. The written report, signed by the medical practitioner or other authorized person responsible, must contain a critical evaluation of all the data collected during the clinical investigation.

What You Need to Know

Dr. D would like to begin this section by reiterating one of his favorite broken-record comments, "Medical device manufacturers need to design, develop, and manufacture devices that are safe and effective." In the eyes of the regulatory folks in the EU, which include the Competent Authorities and their first line of defense, the notified bodies; conformity to essential requirements is mandatory. That being said, clinical investigations provide confirmation that devices are safe and effective in their intended use. As prescribed by Annex X of the Directive, device manufacturers are expected to execute some level of what the doctor appropriately calls "clinical due diligence." Clinical due diligence could be as simple as a critical review and analysis of relevant literature and scientific data for similar or predicate devices, or a full-blown clinical trial. The type of clinical evaluation or investigation will be based in part on the device classification and its intended use. Regardless of the approach, the data will be required to support device application and subsequent approvals. The doctor recommends that device manufacturers work closely with their notified bodies, as they can guide you through the sometimes treacherous regulatory waters associated with entry into the European device market. If a device manufacturer's notified body determines that a clinical investigation will be required to support the submission process, the device manufacturer better start planning for the execution of the actual trials.

In being a bit more specific, the following list captures the types of clinical assessments required by the Directive.

1. The collection of relevant scientific literature and a subsequent critical analysis of this data.

2. The analysis of clinical investigations performed.

3. A combination of number one and number two.

If the device classification steers the device manufacturer, with a gentle nudge from their notified body, to pursue a clinical investigation; there are some basic requirements that need to be considered.

1. Clear objectives of the clinical investigation must be stated, including potential risks.

2. Ethical considerations in accordance with the Helsinki Declaration must be observed (an interesting read).

3. Bribes (just kidding)

4. Methods employed as part of the clinical investigation must be clearly delineated within a written and approved protocol. Some of the considerations are:

   a. The written protocol and supporting documentation shall be appropriate for the device employed in the investigation.

   b. The investigation must be performed in an environment that mimics the expected normal conditions the device will typically be employed.

   c. Device features and performance characteristics must be appropriately examined for safety and efficacy while considering the overall impact to the patient, including risk.

   d. Adverse events must be recorded, and reported to the Competent Authorities immediately, a.k.a., ASAP!

   e. The investigation must be performed by a qualified professional. Dr. Frankenstein or Dr. Jekyll probably do not qualify under the Directive.

   f. A signed written report containing a critical analysis of the clinical investigation and the data collected will be the salient deliverables of the clinical investigation. Without this report, device manufacturers will not be permitted to; "Pass Go and collect their €200.00."

What You Need to Do

As always, Dr. D strongly recommends that device manufacturers hold council with their notified bodies to determine the clinical requirements to support device approvals in the EU. After all, device manufacturers pay significant coin to retain notified bodies, so it is only common sense to include them in the decision making process.

Remember, it will be the notified body that is tasked with reviewing the application, declaration of conformity, technical file or design dossier, and the ultimate determination if conformance to essential requirements has been achieved.

In repeating a key element of the previous section, device manufacturers will need to ensure one of the following scenarios occur.

1. The collection of relevant scientific literature and a subsequent critical analysis of this data.

2. The analysis of clinical investigations performed.

3. A combination of number one and number two.

4. The actual performance of a clinical investigation.

Remember, the expectation of notified bodies and Competent Authorities is that some level of "clinical due diligence" is required to meet the Directive. Typically, Class III device submissions should be supported by data obtained from a well-run clinical investigation. Class IIa and IIb devices, can generally be supported through the collection and critical analysis of scientific data and previous clinical investigations performed. However, Dr. D strongly recommends working with your notified body prior to deciding on the appropriate path to meet the clinical investigation requirement. By the way, did the doctor mention you actually pay your notified bodies? Just kidding, of course I did.

Takeaways

The takeaway for this chapter is eloquently simple. The expectations of the Competent Authorities are that medical devices should always be safe and effective while conformity to essential requirements is achieved. Under Article X of the Directive, safety and efficacy are assessed through the employment of what Dr. D calls, "clinical due diligence." The clinical requirement can be achieved by: (a) the collection and critical analysis of scientific data for similar or predicate devices; (b) a review of clinical investigation data; (c) the actual performance of a clinical investigation; or (d) a combination of a, b, or c.

"Clinical investigations provide confirmation that devices are safe and effective in their intended use."

Chapter 38 – *Annex XI*

"Criteria to be met for the Designation of Notified Bodies"

Chapter Thirty-eight – Annex XI

Annex XI (Criteria to be met for the Designation of Notified Bodies) of Council

Directive 93/42/EEC, a.k.a., the Medical Device Directive (MDD), is all about the

notified bodies. Not unlike that weird aunt or uncle everyone claims to have, device

manufacturers wishing to enter into the European device market must have a notified

body. Yes, I know, bad analogy Dr. D, but hey, this is my book. As the doctor's second

book DG for Compliance with the MDD is nearing its end (one chapter remaining), the

doctor has mentioned the importance of the notified bodies on numerous occasions; and

the importance of selecting one a device manufacturer can work closely with as a partner.

Remember, once a notified body has been selected, this partnership is not unlike a

marriage. A bad marriage, ending in divorce, can be extremely costly to device

manufacturers. Trust Dr. D when I say the pain and costs associated with moving to a

new notified body are significant. That being said, this chapter will dive into the

regulatory responsibilities all notified bodies must fulfill, under Annex XI. One final

thought before diving into Annex XI, some device manufacturers, and you know who

you are, at times attempt to rebel against the onerous requirements of the MDD; however,

the continued contumaciousness (look-it-up) will not result in scoring brownie points

with the notified bodies.

The MDD – 93/42/EEC

ANNEX XI – Criteria to be met for the Designation of Notified Bodies

*1. The notified body, its Director and the assessment and verification staff shall not be
the designer, manufacturer, supplier, installer or user of the devices which they inspect,
nor the authorized representative of any of these persons. They may not be directly
involved in the design, construction, marketing or maintenance of the devices, nor
represent the parties engaged in these activities. This in no way precludes the possibility
of exchanges of technical information between the manufacturer and the body.*

2. The notified body and its staff must carry out the assessment and verification operations with the highest degree of professional integrity and the requisite competence in the field of medical devices and must be free from all pressures and inducements, particularly financial, which might influence their judgment or the results of the inspection, especially from persons or groups of persons with an interest in the results of the verifications.

Should the notified body subcontract specific tasks connected with the establishment and verification of the facts, it must first ensure that the subcontractor meets the provisions of the Directive and, in particular, of this Annex. The notified body shall keep at the disposal of the national authorities the relevant documents assessing the subcontractor's qualifications and the work carried out by the subcontractor under this Directive.

3. The notified body must be able to carry out all the tasks assigned to such bodies by one of Annexes II to VI and for which it has been notified, whether these tasks are carried out by the body itself or on its responsibility. In particular, it must have the necessary staff and possess the facilities needed to perform properly the technical and administrative tasks entailed in assessment and verification. This presupposes the availability of sufficient scientific staff within the organization who possess experience and knowledge sufficient to assess the medical functionality and performance of devices for which it has been notified, having regard to the requirements of this Directive and, in particular, those set out in Annex I. It must also have access to the equipment necessary for the verifications required.

4. The notified body must have:

> — *sound vocational training covering all the assessment and verification operations for which the body has been designated,*

> — *satisfactory knowledge of the rules on the inspections which they carry out and adequate experience of such inspections,*

> — *the ability required to draw up the certificates, records and reports to demonstrate that the inspections have been carried out.*

5. The impartiality of the notified body must be guaranteed. Their remuneration must not depend on the number of inspections carried out, nor on the results of the inspections.

6. The body must take out civil liability insurance, unless liability is assumed by the State under domestic legislation or the Member State itself carries out the inspections directly.

7. The staff of the notified body are bound to observe professional secrecy with regard to all information gained in the course of their duties (except vis-à-vis the competent administrative authorities of the State in which their activities are carried out) pursuant to this Directive or any provision of national law putting it into effect.

What You Need to Know

The good news is that device manufacturers only need to acknowledge that seven basic elements associated with Annex XI exist, since this Annex pertains only to the notified bodies. It is under this Annex, the Competent Authorities can unload a world of pain on notified bodies that fail to meet their regulatory responsibilities under the Directive. One point Dr. D would like to make is that device manufacturers should be auditing their notified bodies to ensure that notified bodies are remaining in compliance with the MDD. Besides, this is an opportunity for device manufacturers to switch up the relationship and place their notified bodies into the "audit hot seat," including the assignment of corrective action, even if it is just for a day. The only downside is that although device manufacturers pay their notified bodies for audits, it is unlikely device manufacturers will be able to extract payment for returning the audit favor.

As stated in the previous section, there are a few salient requirements notified bodies are required to comply with under Annex XI.

1. For starters, notified bodies are not permitted to design, manufacture, supply, install, use, or act as the authorized representative for devices they are tasked with the review and approval. This is what Dr. D calls the proverbial "separation of church and state rule."

2. The staff of the notified body must be qualified to perform accurate assessments on the medical devices they are contracted to review. Financial inducements employed to drive device application approvals, a.k.a., "bribery" is not permitted under the Directive; and will probably result with a number of people being fitted

for orange jumpsuits.

3. Notified bodies must be able to perform their duties as delineated under Annexes II, III, IV, V, and VI. To accomplish these duties, the expectation under the Directive is that notified bodies retain sufficient headcount, equipment, and facilities.

4. Notified bodies must have adequate training, knowledge, and experience, including the ability to create, issue, and manage certificates.

5. The notified body must always be impartial, regardless of the payments received from device manufacturers.

6. The notified body must purchase and retain liability insurance.

7. The notified body must observe appropriate levels of professional secrecy; so Dr. D always recommends having a signed Non-Disclosure Agreement (NDA) in place.

What You Need to Do

By the way, did the doctor mention that device manufacturers must contract with and pay their notified body for their services (just kidding)? From a device manufacturer's perspective, there is really nothing for you to do in regards to Annex XI. Obviously, bribery is out of the question. However, a point Dr. D has made on several occasions must be strongly considered. Device manufacturers need to be choosey when selecting a notified body. This will be a long-term relationship, so selecting a competent and well-recognized notified body should result in excellent support when navigating the European regulatory waters. Although Dr. D is not a paid spokesperson for these organizations, the doctor has worked with TUV-R, BSI, DEKRA, and NSAI. Each of these organizations has extensive experience reviewing applications for market entry into the EU. That being said, whatever the notified body choice, pick one and stick with them. Why? Because changing a notified body mid-stream can be expensive.

Takeaways

The takeaway from this chapter is extremely simple. Device manufactures can take some comfort in knowing that notified bodies are also held to a high standard under the Directive. Trust Dr. D when I say, the Competent Authorities have the ability to turn-up the heat for notified bodies that fail to meet their regulatory obligations under the Directive. Finally, please do not forget to add your notified body to your audit schedule. It is actually quite exhilarating to put the notified body through the ringer during an audit. However, remember the notified bodies are obliged to return the favor once each year, so be gentle.

"Not unlike that weird aunt or uncle everyone claims to have, device manufacturers wishing to enter into the European device market must have a notified body."

Chapter 39 – *Annex XII "CE Marking of Conformity"*

Chapter Thirty-nine – Annex XII

Annex XII (CE Marking of Conformity) of Council Directive 93/42/EEC, a.k.a., the Medical Device Directive (MDD), is all about the Mark, the whole Mark, and nothing but the Mark. All kidding aside, the regulators in the European Union (EU) are very much in love with their CE Mark and frown down upon those who attempt to change it. For those of you that are aficionados of classic rock and roll, would you like to see Led Zeppelin's Stairway to Heaven played as a country music ballad? I am sure that answer is probably a resounding "not a chance!" Well guess what, regulators in the EU do not want to see their CE Mark modified to look like something Pablo Picasso may have painted. Yes, I know - bad analogy Dr. D, but let me repeat, "This is my book." Since Annex XII is by-and-far the shortest Annex, the doctor will focus on a few of the salient requirements to obtain the CE marking of conformity, and equally important, keeping the CE Mark. Dr. D will also provide some brief insight into the design of the CE Mark, the object of Annex XII and this chapter's guidance. As with all of the Doctor's fine prose, I hope the readers will not castigate or threaten defenestration (look-it-up) just because Dr. D's strong opinions may be obverse to the opinions held by some of the readers. Regardless, the doctor hopes you thoroughly enjoy this final chapter, "Devine Guidance for complying with the MDD."

The MDD – 93/42/EEC

ANNEX XII – CE Marking of Conformity

The CE conformity marking shall consist of the initials 'CE' taking the following form:

— *If the marking is reduced or enlarged the proportions given in the above graduated drawing must be respected.*

— *The various components of the CE marking must have substantially the same vertical dimension, which may not be less than 5 mm.*

This minimum dimension maybe waived for small-scale devices.

What You Need to Know

Like Dr. D mentioned in the intro to this Chapter, I will provide some of the salient points associated with the obtainment and retention of the CE marking of conformity.

1. The CE Mark and registration number belong to the notified body. It is through their good graces that device manufacturers have permission to affix the CE Mark to their product.

2. The first step in the CE Mark adventure, apart from developing a medical device that is safe and effective, is to establish a Quality Management System (QMS) that is compliant with ISO 13485:2003.

3. Applications for Class IIa and IIb devices require a technical file to be compiled. Chances are pretty darn good the notified body will want to review the technical file. Long gone are the days of "just trust us" and "self-certification."

4. Applications for Class III devices require a design dossier to be compiled. The notified bodies are required to review the design dossier.

5. The notified bodies will assess a device manufacturer's QMS and issue a certificate stating compliance, if the QMS is deemed in compliance with the standard.

6. Regardless of device classification or rule, medical devices must conform to their established essential requirements. In fact, an Essential Requirements Checklist (ERC) is a salient requirement for all submissions.

7. The Chief Jailable Officer (CJO) will need to review, approve, and sign a Declaration of Conformity (DoC) for each of the devices and/or device families submitted to the notified body for review. A copy of the DoC shall be placed into the technical files and design dossiers.

8. It is a violation of European law to ship medical devices into the EU, for commerce, without a CE Mark.

9. It is a violation of European law to ship medical devices into the EU, for commerce, with a wrongly affixed CE Mark.

10. Device manufacturers are not permitted to affix a CE Mark until all of the appropriate documentation and approvals have been received from their notified body.

11. If it has been determined, through vigilance reporting or some other means, that devices shipped into the EU, are not safe and effective, device manufacturers must take immediate action. The notified body can force the removal of the CE Mark from the offending product.

12. If a device manufacturer fails to maintain their QMS in accordance with ISO 13485:2003; and in accordance with the Annexes of the MDD, the notified body

can force the removal of the CE Mark from product.

13. Finally, no CE Mark means zero (0) medical-device sales revenue coming from the EU, in short, "No Mark, No Money."

Getting back to the CE marking of conformity, the topic of this chapter, there are three basic components associated with Annex XII.

1. If the device manufacture decides to enlarge the CE Mark or shrink the CE Mark, the proportions of the mark must be sustained. In short, device manufactures cannot have: (a) a big C followed by a little E; (b) a little C followed by a big E; (c) a fat C followed by a skinny E; (d) a skinny C followed by a Fat E; (e) or any combination of a through d.

2. The Annex prescribes a minimum vertical dimension of 5 mm for the CE Mark.

3. If it is not possible to meet the 5 mm requirement due to space constraints, the CE Mark can be reduced in size; however, the proportions must be maintained in accordance with bullet-point one (1).

What You Need to Do

Dr. D strongly recommends that the graphic art's folks, supporting a device manufacturers' labeling and packaging functions, get the artwork for the CE Mark correct on the first pass. There is nothing like making a good first impression. Remember, when submitting technical documentation (technical files and design dossiers) to the notified body, they are going to want to review the labeling. Labeling will include the device carton (box) label, device pouch label, and the Instructions for Use (IFU), as appropriate. If the CE Mark is wrong, it will be back to the drawing board. Another Dr. D watch-out pertains to device manufacturers that employ multiple notified bodies. Make sure the correct CE Mark is placed on the correct product. Nothing says were out of control more than misbranded product. Simple stated; the placement of the wrong CE Mark, onto the wrong product, is considered misbranding.

Takeaways

From this chapter, the message is quite clear. The regulatory gods in the EU like their CE marking of conformity just as the mark is depicted in Annex XII. There is no need to improve on the already perceived perfection in mark design. In fact to do so, is a violation of the Directive. The size and proportion requirements for the CE marking of conformity are clearly depicted in Annex XII. Dr. D's best advice is to abide by the Annex and leave perfection alone.

"The regulators in the European Union (EU) are very much in love with their CE Mark and frown down upon those who attempt to change it."

Epilogue

Epilogue

As one of my favorite Warner Brother's cartoon characters used to say; "That's all folks." Thank you Bugs Bunny or should I say Mel Blanc. Regardless, 279-pages later; and this guidance has come to an end. That being said, I hope you have enjoyed reading the prose of Dr. D and garnered some useful knowledge from the book. At the end of the day, ongoing compliance to the MDD does pose a significant challenge; however, compliance is achievable by simply doing the right things. One of the trends that the doctor continues to find disturbing is the perception that the MDD is perceived as something less than law. Granted, the notified bodies and the Competent Authorities have a different approach in regards to assessing the compliance of device manufacturers and the enforcement of regulatory non-conformances. It is the opinion held by Dr. D and other industry professionals, the approach and touch of the regulatory bodies in Europe are much gentler than those of the FDA. However, make no mistake, the MDD is the law for all 27-Member States (as of this book); and they take the law very seriously.

In closing, Dr. D would like to leave you with a few salient points (Dr. D's commandments for compliance with the MDD) that should help guide you through your daily quality and regulatory lives.

1. Never take shortcuts in regards to the Quality Management System (QMS). Once the QMS has been approved ensure that it is monitored, reviewed, revised, and maintained, in a constant of compliance.

2. Use the QMS tools such as internal audits and CAPA to keep the QMS in compliance.

3. Selection of a qualified notified body should be considered a mission critical activity. Treat like a marriage; hopefully a good marriage because the notified body is the portal into the European device market.

4. Always design, develop, and manufacture, quality medical devices. If a medical device cannot be deemed safe and effective in its intended use, well what is the point?

5. Make sure all medical devices and the processes employed to build them and properly verified and/or validated.

6. Compiling technical files (Class IIa & IIb) and design dossiers (Class III) for review and approval by the notified bodies is only half of the regulatory challenge. Ensure this technical documentation is properly maintained for the life of the product (plus 5 or 15 years depending on the device).

7. The CE marking of conformity must be placed onto the packaging of all approved medical devices shipped into the EU.

8. Never wrongly affix a CE Mark to unapproved product.

9. Maintain an effective post-market surveillance system to address customer complaints and vigilance reports. If a medical device is hurting the user or the patient, do not hesitate to pull it from the market.

10. All medical devices require a signed Declaration of Conformity (DoC) as part of the submission process. Ensure the Chief Jailable Officer signs the DoC.

In closing, cheers from Dr. D and best wishes for continued professional success.

"Dr. D"

References

References

AAMI. (2011, February). Association for the Advancement of Medical Instrumentation. Retrieved February 7, 2011, from http://www.aami.org/

Code of Federal Regulation. (2010, April). *Title 21 Part 820: Quality system regulation.* Washington, D.C.: U. S. Government Printing Office.

Council Directive 89/686/EEC. (1989, December). *Council Directive 89/686/EEC on the approximation of the laws of the member states relating to personal protective equipment.* Retrieved January 11, 2011, from http://www.emerigogroup.com

Council Directive 93/42/EEC. (1993, June). *Council Directive 93/42/EEC concerning medical devices.* Retrieved December 21, 2010, from http://eur-lex.europa.eu

Council Directive 96/29/EURATOM. (1996, May). *Council Directive 96/29/EURATOM – laying down basic safety standards for protection of the health of workers and the general public against the dangers arising from ionizing radiation.* Retrieved January 7, 2011, from http://eur-lex.europa.eu

Council Directive 97/43/EURATOM. (1997, June). *Council Directive 97/43/Euratom of 30 June 1997 on health protection of individuals against the dangers of ionizing radiation in relation to medical exposure, and repealing Directive 84/466/Euratom.* Retrieved December 21, 2010, from http://eur-lex.europa.eu

Devine. C. (2009, July). *Exploring the effectiveness of defensive-receiving inspection for medical device manufacturers: a mixed method study.* Published doctoral dissertation. Northcentral University. Prescott Valley, AZ.

Directive 2001/83/EC. (2001, November). *Directive 2001/83/EC of the European Parliament and of the Council of 6 November 2001 on the community code relating to medicinal products for human use.* Retrieved January 7, 2011, from http://www.edctp.org

Directive 2004/108/EC. (2004, December). *Directive 2004/108/EC of the European Parliament and of the Council of 15 December 2004 on the approximation of the laws of the member states relating to electromagnetic compatibility and repealing Directive 89/336/EC.* Retrieved January 7, 2011, from http://eur-lex.europa.eu

Directive 2007/47/EC. (2007, September). *Directive 2007/47/EEC of the European Parliament and of the Council of 5 September 2007 amending Council Directive 90/385/EEC on the approximation of the laws of member states relating to active implantable medical devices, Council Directive 93/42/EEC concerning medical devices and Directive 98//8/EC concerning the placing of biocidal products on the market.* Retrieved December 21, 2010, from http://eur-lex.europa.eu

EN 980:2008. (2008, July). *Symbols to be used in the labeling of medical devices.*

EN ISO 13485:2003. (2004, February). *Medical devices – quality management systems – requirements for regulatory purposes (ISO 13485:2003).*

EN ISO 14971:2009. (2010, March). *Medical devices – application of risk management to medical devices (ISO 14971:2009).*

EUDAMED. (2010, June). *European databank on medical devices.* Retrieved April 25, 2011, from http://ec.europa.eu/consumers/sectors/medical-devices/market-surveillance-vigilance/eudamed/

ISTA. (2011, February). International Safe Transit Association. Retrieved February 7, 2011, from http://www.ista.org/

Is your company ready for the 2010 Medical Device Directives? (2008, June). Medical Design. Retrieved December 22, 2010, from http://medicaldesign/mag/company_ready_medical_0608/

MEDEV 2.12-1 rev 5. (2007, April). *Guidelines on a medical devices vigilance system.* European Commission DG Enterprise and Industry. Retrieved February 26, 2011, from www.**gtlaw.com**/portalresource/lookup/wosid/contentpilot

Medical Device Directive. (1993). Council Directive 93/42/EEC. *Medical Device Safety Service.* Retrieved December 21, 2010, from http://directive93-42-eec.htm

Medical Devices Directive. (2010). Conformance CE Marking and product safety consultancy. Retrieved December 22, 2010, from http://www.conformance.co.uk.

MDD, the Medical Device Directive 93/42/EEC – introduction. (2010). Medical Device Certification. Retrieved December 22, 2010, from http://www.mdc-ce.de/cert_md1.htm

Safety first: reprocessing of medical devices in Europe. (2011, April). European Association of Medical Device Reprocessing. Retrieved April 1, 2011, from http://www.eamdr.org/

Schnoll, L. (1997, September). *The CE Mark: Medical Device Directive.* Retrieved December 22. 2010, from http://www.qualitydigest.com

Third-party medical device reprocessing. (2011, April). Association of Medical Device Reprocessors Website. Retrieved April 1, 2011, from http://www.amdr.org/

Vigilance Reports. (2011, February). Europa.en Website. Retrieved February 26, 2011, from http://ec.europa.eu/consumers/sectors/medical-devices/documents/vigilance-reports/index_en.htm

Made in the USA
Lexington, KY
11 June 2013